Turkish Harems & Circassian Homes

Andrée Hope

Alpha Editions

This edition published in 2024

ISBN : 9789362519399

Design and Setting By
Alpha Editions
www.alphaedis.com
Email - info@alphaedis.com

As per information held with us this book is in Public Domain.
This book is a reproduction of an important historical work. Alpha Editions uses the best technology to reproduce historical work in the same manner it was first published to preserve its original nature. Any marks or number seen are left intentionally to preserve its true form.

Contents

PREFACE. ....- 1 -
CHAPTER I. THE CITY OF THE SUN. ....- 2 -
CHAPTER II. THE HOUR OF PRAYER. ....- 11 -
CHAPTER III. SECTS. ....- 19 -
CHAPTER IV. THE HAREM. ....- 25 -
CHAPTER V. THE HAPPY VALLEY ....- 36 -
CHAPTER VI. AN EASTERN BANQUET. ....- 43 -
CHAPTER VII. EUPATORIA. ....- 48 -
CHAPTER VIII. SEVASTOPOL. ....- 54 -
CHAPTER IX. TRACES OF WAR. ....- 60 -
CHAPTER X. VALLEY OF TCHERNAIA. ....- 68 -
CHAPTER XI. A RUSSIAN INTERIOR. ....- 74 -
CHAPTER XII. CIRCASSIA. ....- 86 -
CHAPTER XIII. SOUKOUM. ....- 92 -
CHAPTER XIV. CIRCASSIAN MEN AND WOMEN. ....- 103 -
CHAPTER XV. A LAST RIDE. ....- 111 -
CHAPTER XVI. SINOPE. ....- 116 -
CHAPTER XVII. STORM-CLOUDS. ....- 124 -

PREFACE.

It is hoped by the Authoress that this little record of a past summer may recall some pleasant recollections to those who have already visited the sunny lands she attempts to describe; and that her accounts, though they inadequately express the beauty and charm of these distant countries, may interest those who prefer travelling for half-an-hour when seated in their arm-chairs.

CHAPTER I.
THE CITY OF THE SUN.

It was on a sunny summer morning that an English schooner yacht, that had been tossing about all night on the stormy waves of the Sea of Marmora, rounded the point opposite Scutari, and, gracefully spreading her wings like a white bird, came rapidly on under the influence of the fresh morning breeze, and cast anchor at the entrance of the Golden Horn.

The rattle of the chain had scarcely ceased when up came all the poor sea-sick folk from below, for yachting people can be sea-sick sometimes, whatever may be the popular belief to the contrary.

Never, perhaps, was a greater Babel of tongues heard on board any little vessel. The owner of the yacht, his wife and sister, were English; but there was an Italian governess, a French maid, a German bonne, a Neapolitan captain, a Maltese mate, two children speaking indifferently well most of these languages, and a crew comprising every nation bordering the Mediterranean.

(This little explanation has been given in excuse for the desultory nature of the few pages that are offered, with much diffidence, to a kind public, as they consist principally of extracts from the journals and letters of the various dwellers on board the *Claymore*.)

Besides these many tongues that were pouring forth expressions of joy and admiration with a vehemence of gesticulation and an energy of tone unknown in northern lands, two canaries, gifted with the most vigorous lungs and the most indefatigable throats, lifted up their shrill voices to add to the general clamour.

All this uproar, however, was but to express the delight every one felt at the unequalled beauty of the scene before them.

"Veder Napoli, e poi morir!" is a well-known saying. Put Constantinople instead of Naples, and the flattering words are equally applicable.

Constantinople has been so often written about that it is useless to describe its lovely aspect in detail. Every one knows that there are minarets and towers rising up, in fairy-like grace, from amid gardens and cypress groves; but "he who would see it aright" should have his first view in all the bright unreality of a sunny summer morning. Soon after dawn, in the tender duskiness of the early hours, when the light steals down shyly from the veiled east, and before the business and noise of a great city begin, Constantinople is like the sleeping beauty in the wood. A great hush is over everything, broken only when the sun comes up in a blaze of light, flooding sea, earth, and city with a "glory" of life and colour.

Then from each minaret is heard the voice of the muezzins, as they summon the faithful to prayers. The fairy-like caïques skim in every direction across the waters; and the beautifully-named but dirty and somewhat ugly Golden Horn is all astir with moving vessels.

Nearly opposite the yacht was a very handsome building of white Greek marble, with an immense frontage to the sea. This is the Sultan's palace of Dolmé-Batché. The wing on the right, where the windows are closely barred and jealously latticed, contains the apartments of the ladies of the Imperial harem.

Behind the palace, stretching up the hill and crowning its summit, are seen the white, handsome houses that form the fashionable suburb of Pera. Here ambassadors and bankers have large, comfortable hotels; here, too, are the European shops, and the promenade for the Christian world. But the part to see—the part that interests—is, of course, the old Turkish quarter, Stamboul; for in Stamboul are Turks in turbans, and in Stamboul are real Turkish houses.

More tumble-down places it would be difficult to find. A man had need to be a fatalist to live in a house of which all the four walls lean at different angles. A fire, instead of a misfortune, must be a real blessing, were it only to bring some air into the dirty, narrow, ill-savoured streets.

The dirt, the narrowness, and the wretchedly bad pavement, combined with another trouble, the multitude of dogs lying about, make walking, pain and grief to the newly-arrived foreigner.

Besides these disagreeables, there is the danger of being crushed flat against a wall by human beasts of burden called "hamals" or porters. It is really frightful to see men so laden.

As they come staggering along, bent double beneath their loads, at every few steps they utter a loud cry, to warn passers-by to get out of their way. It is, however, by no means an easy matter to avoid them. The streets are so narrow and tortuous that, after jumping hastily aside to escape one monstrous package coming up the road, the unhappy stranger is nearly knocked over by another huge load coming down. Dogs' tails, too, are always lying where dogs' tails should not be; and in the agitation and anxiety caused by incessantly darting from side to side of the street to avoid the groaning "hamals," it is exceedingly difficult to avoid treading occasionally on one of these inconvenient tails, and then the whole quarter resounds with hideous howlings.

The bazaars have been so well and so fully described that it is needless to say much about them. Our first sensation on seeing them was, perhaps, that of a little disappointment; but after a time we better appreciated the picturesque beauty and richness of colouring that the long dark lanes of little shops presented.

As a rule, few pretty things, excepting shoes and slippers, are exposed on the stalls. Rugs, carpets, shawls, and jewels are generally kept behind the shops in cupboards and warehouses.

Turquoises were very abundant and low in price, but all we saw were of inferior quality, and the large stones had some flaw. Pretty melon-shaped caskets are made in silver to hold cakes, and the silver rose-water bottles are charming both in design and workmanship. Foreigners are speedily attracted to the drug bazaar by the odd mixture of pungent, pleasant, and disagreeable odours that proceed from it. Here the scene is like a living picture of the "Arabian Nights' Tales." Like Amine in the story of "The Three Calenders," many a veiled figure attended by her black slave may be seen making her purchases of drugs and spices of the venerable old doctors, who, with spectacles on nose, and huge musty folios at their side, look the very personification of wisdom, equally able to administer medicines and to draw the horoscopes of their patients.

The arms bazaar is also attractive, not only for the magnificence and value of its contents, but from the picturesque beauty of the quaint, dark, lofty old building in which the richly-decorated weapons are displayed.

At first, the immense amount of bargaining that is required before any purchase can be effected is very amusing; but after some weeks it becomes tiresome, even to people who have had many years' experience in Italy.

If anything of importance has to be bought, many hours, sometimes many days, elapse between the opening of the business and its conclusion.

The friends of both parties cordially assist in the affair with the utmost force of their lungs, and an amount of falsehood is told by Christians as well as Turks that ought to lie heavily on the consciences of all; but "do in Turkey as the Turks do," is a maxim which all appear to accept, and so no one dreams of speaking the truth in a Constantinople bazaar.

When the struggle is at its height, coffee is brought, which materially recruits the strength of all concerned, and should the affair be very important, a friendly pipe is smoked; then everyone sets to work again, vowing, protesting, denying. The seller asserts by all that is holy that he will lose money, but that such is the love he feels for the stranger and the Frank, that he will sell the article to him for such and such a price (probably four times as much as the sum he means to take), and at length, after an exhausting afternoon, the foreigner retires triumphant, bearing away with him the coveted shawls or carpets, and not having paid perhaps more than double the money they are worth.

As we remained on the Bosphorus for a considerable part of the summer, we were enabled not only to see at our ease the many objects of interest to be found in Constantinople and the lovely country that surrounds it, but also to gratify the great wish we had of becoming somewhat acquainted with Turkish life, and of learning something of the realities of Turkish homes.

Every year it is more difficult for passing travellers to gain admittance to the harems. Of course the members of the principal families object to be made a show of, and equally of course the wives of the diplomatists residing in Constantinople are unwilling to intrude too frequently upon the privacy of these ladies. A Turkish visit also entails a somewhat serious loss of time, as it generally lasts from mid-day to sunset.

When royal and other very great ladies arrive at Constantinople, certain grand fêtes are given to them in different official houses, but these magnificent breakfasts and dinners do not give Europeans a better knowledge of Turkish homes than a dinner or ball at Buckingham Palace or the Tuileries would give a Turk respecting the nature of domestic life in England or France.

The wives of several diplomats had given us letters of introduction to many of their friends at Constantinople, and so kindly were these responded to by the Turkish ladies that we found ourselves received at once with the greatest cordiality, and before we left the shores of the Bosphorus had made friendships that we heartily trust we may be fortunate enough to renew at some future day.

After a stay of several months, our conviction was that it would be difficult to find people more kind-hearted, more simple-mannered, or more sweet-tempered than the Turkish women.

The servants, or slaves, are treated with a kindness and consideration that many Christian households would do well to imitate. They seem quite part of the family, and in fact a woman slave does belong to it should she have a child, as she then is entitled to her freedom, and her master is bound to accord her certain privileges which give her a position higher than that of a servant, though she does not attain the dignity of being a wife.

The greatest punishment we have heard of, and which is only inflicted on viragos whose tongues set the whole harem in a flame, is to *sell* (or what is still worse) to *give* them away to a family of inferior rank.

This is considered a frightful indignity, and one which, when seriously threatened, usually suffices to still the veriest shrew.

Of course a jealous and perhaps neglected wife may occasionally make a pretty young odalisk's life somewhat uncomfortable, but harsh usage and cruelty are almost unknown; and in general the wife (for now there is seldom more than one) is quite satisfied if her authority is upheld, and if she remain the supreme head of the household. If content on these matters, she rarely troubles herself about the amusements of her husband.

A Turkish woman also rapidly becomes old, and after a few years of youth finds her principal happiness in the care of her children, in eating, in the gossip at the bath, and in the weekly drive to the Valley of the Sweet Waters.

A Turkish wife, whatever her rank, is always at home at sunset to receive her husband, and to present him with his pipe and slippers when, his daily work over, he comes to enjoy the repose of his harem.

In most households also the wife superintends her husband's dinner, and has the entire control over all domestic affairs.

The greatest charm of the Turkish ladies consists in the perfect simplicity of their manners, and in the total absence of all pretence.

When we knew them better, the childlike frankness with which they talked was both amusing and pleasant; but many of them nevertheless were shrewd and intelligent, and had they received anything like adequate education, would have been able to compete with some of the most talented of their European sisters.

As mothers, their tenderness is unequalled, but their fault here is over-indulgence of the children, who, until ten or twelve years of age, are permitted to do everything they like.

Many of the ladies whose acquaintance we made showed a remarkably quick ear, and great facility in learning various songs and pieces of music that we gave them. Their voices were sweet and melodious, and it was surprising with what rapidity they caught the Italian and Neapolitan airs that they heard us sing.

The great bar to any real progress being made towards their due education, and the enlargement of their minds, is the seclusion in which they live.

Men and women are evidently not intended to live socially apart, for each deteriorates by the separation. Men who live only with other men become rough, selfish, and coarse; whilst women, when entirely limited to the conversation of their own sex, grow indolent, narrow-minded, and scandal-loving. Like flint and steel, the brilliant spark only comes forth when the necessary amount of friction has been applied.

Whatever degree of intimacy may be attained, it is rare that foreigners obtain a knowledge of more than the surface of Turkish life and manners. Strangers, therefore, should speak with much caution and reserve; but still, even a casual observer must perceive that polygamy and the singular laws regarding succession are productive of innumerable evils amongst the Turks.

The men, it is said, have but little, if any, love for their offspring. Not only do they dislike the expense of bringing up children, but fathers dread having sons who in time may become their most dangerous enemies.

In quiet families who live apart from public life the boys have a better chance of being spared. In families of very high rank but few are to be seen, whilst in the households of the relatives of the Sultan they are still more rare.

Infanticide, therefore, prevails extensively; it is hinted at without scruple; in fact, the Turks, both men and women, do not hesitate to express their surprise that Europeans encumber themselves with large families.

In the Imperial House, the throne descends in succession to each son of a deceased Sultan before any grandson can inherit. This regulation was made in order that the monarch should be the nearest living relative of the Prophet.

In olden times, therefore, the first act of a Sultan on ascending the throne was to get rid of all his brothers by imprisonment or death, not only for the purpose of securing the crown for his own children, but to prevent the risk that might accrue to himself by there being a grown-up successor ready to usurp his place.

Personal merit used to be a matter of comparative indifference to the Turks, provided the Sultan were a member of the great imperial family. Occasionally therefore monarchs, who had reason to believe themselves much hated by their subjects, have not hesitated to sacrifice their own offspring to their fears.

The late Sultan, Abd-ul-Medjid, was thought a wonder of liberality because he permitted his brother, the present Sultan, to live. But Abd-ul-Medjid's heart had been softened by a sorrow he had had in early life. Shortly before he came to the throne he had a favourite odalisk, to whom he was much attached. In those days none of the royal princes were permitted to become fathers, and the poor girl fell a sacrifice to the State policy which forbade her becoming the mother of a living child. Within a week of her death Sultan Mahmoud died, and his son ascended the throne. Had the odalisk lived and had a son, she would have enjoyed the rank of first "Kadun" to the reigning monarch.

The Sultan's rank is so elevated—his position is so far above that of every other mortal—that there is no woman on earth sufficiently his equal to enable him to marry her. He has, therefore, no legal wife, but his ladies are called "Kaduns," or companions, and the mother of his eldest son is always chief kadun, a position that gives her many advantages. These ladies are not called sultanas, for only the princesses of the blood-royal enjoy that title, but the mother of the reigning sovereign is named Sultan-Validé.

Occasionally, when there is a subject whom the Sultan wishes especially to honour, the favoured pasha has one of the monarch's daughters or sisters given to him in marriage; but this great distinction is sometimes the cause of much sorrow, and uproots much domestic happiness, as all other wives must be sent away, and the children of such marriages equally banished, before the royal bride will condescend to enter the pasha's harem. Even after marriage, the royal lady will sometimes insist upon retaining all the privileges of her rank, and in that case the husband becomes the veriest slave imaginable, never daring to enter the harem unless summoned by the princess, and when there often obliged to remain standing while receiving the orders of his imperial and imperious wife. F—— Pasha, though his ambition was gratified by becoming the brother-in-law of the Sultan, paid somewhat dearly, if reports be true, for the honour of this royal alliance, as the princess was said to be a lady of uncertain temper, or rather of a very certain temper, as Charles Dickens described it. At any rate F—— Pasha's heart clung to the forsaken wife and children of his humbler and perhaps happier days; and sometimes in the dusk of the evening a small, undecorated caïque, containing a man closely muffled up, might be seen darting swiftly across the Bosphorus from the palace of the lordly pasha to the remote quarter of Scutari, where, in a humble house in a back street, were hid away the poor deserted wife and her little children.

All, therefore, is not gold that glitters in the lives of the members of the imperial family, and the State policy that ordains there shall not be too many heirs near the throne often wrings the heart and embitters the existence of many of the tender-hearted princesses.

Although the men probably accept the necessities of this policy with comparative indifference, the mothers do not so easily resign themselves to the loss of their infants, and many a sad story gets whispered about of the grievous struggles some of the poor creatures have made to preserve their little ones from the impending doom.

The death of one royal lady that took place while we were at Constantinople, was hastened by the grief she had gone through by thus losing her only boy.

When her marriage took place, she had obtained the promise that all her children were to be spared. In due time a boy was born, and the father received an intimation that the child had better "cease to be." The Sultana, however, claimed the fulfilment of the promise that had been made her, and watched and guarded the little fellow most rigorously.

The Sultan's word being inviolable, it was not possible to break it openly, but the mother was aware of the jealousy that was created by the privilege accorded to her, and knew that the child's life was in constant peril. It is said that attempts were made both to poison and to drown him, but these cruel designs were frustrated by the vigilance of his mother, who never suffered the child to be absent from her.

When the boy was between two and three years old, two more of the Sultan's daughters married, and many magnificent fêtes were given on the occasion. The elder sister was of course present, accompanied as usual by her little son; but one day in the crowd the child disappeared, and has never since been heard of.

Although the poor mother had another child, a girl, she never held up her head again after the disappearance of her boy, and actually pined away and died from grief at his loss.

This is not a solitary instance of the sorrows of royal Turkish ladies.

As we became more intimate with the inhabitants of the harem, and were able to understand and express ourselves a little better, our friends made themselves very merry at the expense of some of our Frank customs. Few of our habits appeared to them more ludicrous than that of the men so incessantly raising their hats.

When quarrelling, it is a common mode of abuse to say, "May your fatigued and hated soul, when it arrives in purgatory, find no more rest than a Giaour's hat enjoys on earth!"

The Turkish language is rich and euphonious, and is capable of so much variety of expression that it is remarkably well adapted to poetry. The verses we occasionally heard recited had a rhythm that was exceedingly agreeable to the ear.

Though improvements do not march on in Turkey with giant strides, still progress is being made surely, though slowly; and many of the Turks, besides being well educated in other respects, now speak Italian, English, and French with much fluency. Some of the ladies, also, are beginning to learn these languages, although most of them, excepting those very few who have been abroad, are too shy to venture to speak in a foreign tongue.

The Sultan's mother—the Sultan-Validé—was a very superior woman, and did much good service towards promoting education. Amongst other of her excellent deeds, she founded a college for the instruction of young candidates for public offices.

There are now in Constantinople medical, naval, and agricultural schools, all well attended, and fairly well looked after.

For the women, private tuition is of course their only means of learning, and not only is the supply of governesses very limited, but their abilities are in general of a very mediocre description.

Unless in very superior families, a little—a very little Arabic, to enable them to read, though not to understand, the Koran, working, knitting, and perhaps a slight acquaintance with French and music, is deemed amply sufficient knowledge for daughters to acquire.

CHAPTER II.
THE HOUR OF PRAYER.

There is much that is both grand and poetical in many of the practices of the Mohammedan religion; and few things strike the stranger more than the frequent calls to prayer that resound at certain hours of the day from every minaret of the city.

The formula used is simple, but heart-stirring: "Allah akbar! Allah akbar! Great God! Great God! There is no God but God! I declare that Mohammed is the apostle of God! O great Redeemer! O Ruler of the universe! Great God! Great God! There is no God but God."

This is chanted by the muezzin in a loud but musical voice as he walks slowly around the minaret, thus summoning from every portion of the globe the faithful to join him in holy prayer.

At sunrise, at mid-day, at three o'clock, and again at nine, the sacred cry re-echoes above the city, and every true believer as it reaches his ear prostrates himself with his face towards Mecca, exclaiming: "There is no power, no might, but in God Almighty."

All who can, perform their devotions in the mosques, although earnest prayer is quite as efficacious when made in a house or by the road-side.

One Friday, having provided ourselves with the necessary firman, we repaired to Santa Sophia, and arrived there a few minutes before the hour of mid-day prayer. Franks are now admitted into the mosque, but have to put on slippers over their boots, that they may not defile the exquisite cleanliness of the floor. As the service was about to begin, we went up to one of the galleries, and from thence had a good general view of the interior.

Nothing could be more simple. There was as little decoration as would be found in a low-church Protestant chapel. A few ostrich eggs and some large candelabra hung from the roof, but all the Christian paintings and ornaments have been destroyed or defaced. The figures and the six wings of the famous cherubim can still be seen faintly traced on the dome, but the faces of the angels have been covered with golden plates, as the Turks interpret very literally the commandment against idolatry.

Although there was but little to see in the mosque itself apart from its historical associations, the vast assemblage of worshippers that nearly filled its spacious area was most interesting to behold.

Stamboul (in which quarter is Santa Sophia) is now principally inhabited by old-fashioned Turks, and by large colonies of Circassians. Many of the worshippers, therefore, wore the flowing robe and stately turban now nearly banished from the more fashionable parts of the town. The Circassians also were habited in their picturesque national costume, and it would be impossible to see anywhere men more dignified or noble in appearance than these poor exiles.

The service is impressive from its grand simplicity. As the hour of noon is proclaimed, the Imaun places himself before a small niche called the Mihrab, that points towards Mecca, and in a loud voice proclaims, "Allah akbar! Allah akbar!" The congregation arise, respond with the same words, and the cry seems, like a mighty wave, to roll backward and forward through the vast space.

Every man then turns his eyes humbly to the ground as the Imaun recites the Fatiha or Lord's Prayer:

"In the name of the most merciful God; praise be to God the Lord of all creatures, the most merciful, the Lord of the Day of Judgment. Thee do we worship, and of Thee do we beg help, direct us in the right way. Direct us in the way of those to whom Thou hast been gracious; not of those against whom thou art incensed, nor of those who go astray. Ameen, ameen!"

The congregation then prostrate themselves repeatedly in acknowledgment of the Almighty's power and might. A chapter of the Koran is read, followed by more prostrations, with another prayer in which the worshippers join. Then the Imaun calls out in a loud voice that each man is to make his private prayer, and the solemn silence and perfect quiet that ensues is most impressive.

Prayers were now over, and those who wished retired. The remainder approached nearer a small pulpit into which another Imaun mounted, who, seated cross-legged on a cushion, commenced an exposition of some portion of the Koran.

No women had hitherto been present during the service, but a few now entered and seated themselves behind the men.

When we walked round the mosque to examine it in detail, we were shown the mark said to have been made by the hand of Sultan Mahmoud when he placed it upon one of the great columns in token that he took possession of the stronghold of the Christian faith. As the spot indicated, however, is at least fifteen feet from the ground, we permitted ourselves to doubt the accuracy of the statement.

After leaving Santa Sophia we passed through the largest square in Constantinople, called Ak' Meidan, or the "place of meat." Here it was that the Janissaries were put to death by the orders of Sultan Mahmoud. This wholesale massacre, fearful as it was, and cruel as it seemed, nevertheless delivered Turkey from one of its greatest scourges, for such was the rapacity, the cruelty, and the overbearing insolence of these famous troops, that no man's life or property was safe for an hour, and the whole country groaned under a tyranny more oppressive than any it had ever known.

After Santa Sophia, the finest mosque in Constantinople is that of Sultan Ahmed. It is a large and handsome building; its six tall, graceful minarets giving much beauty to the exterior, whilst the interior is chiefly remarkable for the eleven gigantic columns that support the roof. The mosque possesses some very fine Korans all richly bound in velvet, some of them even encrusted with pearls and precious stones. There is also a magnificent collection of jewelled cups that have been presented by various sultans and by many rich pashas.

When we issued forth from the cool freshness of the shady mosque, the burning glare of the sun seemed doubly oppressive. We were thankful even to climb into the little telega that was awaiting us; fleas and tight squeezing seeming slight evils compared with the scorching heat and blinding vividness of the sun's rays.

When we halted at the beautiful fountain of Ahmed the Third, never did water and marble look more delicious and refreshing.

This celebrated fountain is one of the most beautiful little buildings in Constantinople. It is an octagon made of white marble, the projecting roof extending far beyond the walls. Where gilt lattice-work has not been let into the sides they are covered with inscriptions in gold letters, extolling the virtues of the treasure it contains; for the waters of the Fountain of Ahmed are said to excel in freshness and purity even those of the Holy Well of the Prophet at Mecca, and have been in many poems compared to the Sacred Fount whose eternal spring has its rise in Paradise itself.

On a little marble slab outside the building are arranged rows of brass cups full of the fresh water so precious to the hot and weary passenger in Constantinople.

As we lingered in the grateful shade, thankful to escape, even for a few minutes, from the scorching heat, two poor hamals came staggering down the street, bent nearly double beneath their terrible loads. With almost a groan of relief they came beneath the shelter of the projecting roof, and, dropping their packs, seated themselves on the fresh, cool marble pavement. It was now three o'clock, and, pouring a few cups of water over their hands and feet, they prostrated themselves towards Mecca, and remained an instant in silent prayer.

These poor fellows, notwithstanding their galling toil, are a merry, contented race of people. From dawn to sunset they work like beasts of burden, and are satisfied with food that would kill an English workman in a week. Our two neighbours each pulled a very small bit of black bread from his pocket, got a slice of melon from an adjacent fruit stall, and this slender fare, washed down by a few cups of water, made their dinner for the day. The repast, slight as it was, was eaten with a cheerfulness and satisfaction that might have been envied by many a gourmand.

At sunset, however, they feel themselves amply repaid for the fatigues of the day if they can but gain enough to indulge in an infinite number of cups of the strongest coffee, which, with the soothing pipe, gives them strength to sustain their prodigious toil.

One ought to visit the East to appreciate, to its full extent, the blessing of an abundance of fresh and pure water. No wonder that the Prophet says that he who bestows the treasure of a fountain on his fellow-men shall be sustained by the supporting hand of the Angel of Mercy as he traverses the perilous bridge made of a single hair, by which alone the gates of Paradise can be reached.

Fresh springs of water, also, are doubly dear to the hearts of the faithful, as by the direct miracle of sending water in the wilderness was the life of Ishmael saved when Sarai succeeded in having the child and his mother Hagar banished from the tents of Abraham.

Wandering far into the recesses of the desert, the small bottle of water with which she had been provided speedily became empty, and the sorrowing and forsaken woman found herself in the terrible wilderness alone, and far from the aid of man. She placed her hapless infant beneath some shrubs, and, retiring to a distance that she might not see the little creature die, the unhappy mother lifted up her voice and wept.

But when was the Almighty deaf to the cry of the afflicted and oppressed? He hears when men's ears and hearts are closed; and, swift as thought, the Angel of Compassion, that watches day and night at the foot of God's throne, sped from his heavenly post and touched the barren earth. The faint flutter of the angel's wings roused the poor mother from her grief: she turned and beheld, gushing brightly from the rock, the stream whose crystal waters brought salvation to herself and to her child.

Although it is the custom to inveigh energetically against the folly of seeing too many sights at once, yet old travellers know full well that no town is really enjoyable until all the wonders of it have been visited.

Then, and not till then, is there rest for mind and body, as, all necessary sights seen, the traveller can seek again the especial objects of his fancy, and in peace and ease make more intimate acquaintance with the scenes of nature, or of art, that have the most charm for him.

Most people, probably, will acknowledge that the former have a considerable supremacy over the latter in Constantinople. There are no picture-galleries, and, excepting some of the mosques, a few palaces, and the Seraglio, there are few buildings to interest a lover of architecture.

The Seraglio, however, is well worth a visit, for, though neither grand, nor beautiful, it is interesting in many ways; and the position it occupies on rising ground at the entrance of the Golden Horn (thus commanding the Bosphorus both east and west) makes the views from its gardens quite unequalled in beauty.

The summer was unusually hot, so that it was often quite an effort to tear ourselves away from the cool rooms and delightful garden of the Embassy at Therapia, where we were staying, and undertake a regular afternoon of sight-seeing, especially also as it was necessary to go to Stamboul, or Pera, in one of the hot little steamers that ply incessantly up and down the Bosphorus.

One intensely hot day, however, we set off for the Seraglio, and the thermometer being at any number of degrees, and the deck of the steamer so crowded that there was barely standing room, we arrived at the gate of the Palace in a very exhausted state. When we entered the first court therefore, and found ourselves under the shade of a gigantic plane-tree, a faint breeze every now and then rustling amongst the leaves, the change was so pleasant that we thought we would give up sight seeing, and stay there till night.

Not only was the cool shade very grateful to our feelings, but the pretty scene before us was very pleasant to the eyes. Beneath the tree was a small fountain, its stream trickling into a shallow marble basin, and on its brink were seated groups of gaily-dressed women, chattering merrily as they ate melon and sweetmeats.

Having never been in Spain, we are ignorant of the witching grace bestowed upon the fair or unfair Spaniard by the magic folds of the mantilla; but not having had that good fortune, we all agreed that no head-dress is so becoming to the female face as the Turkish veil, worn as it is arranged at Constantinople.

Great art and much consideration are bestowed upon the arrangement of the folds; and in this respect a lady of Constantinople is as much superior to her Eastern compeers as a "lionne" in Paris would be above her provincial rivals.

So coquettishly is the transparent muslin folded over the nose and mouth, so tenderly does it veil the forehead, that the delicate cloud seems but to heighten and increase each charm. Far, very far is it from hiding the features from the profaning gaze of man, as was so savagely ordained by Mohammed.

Nose, mouth, and forehead being thus softly shadowed, the great luminous eyes shine out with doubled brilliancy and effect.

It is some consolation to Frank ladies to know that, excepting that never-to-be-sufficiently praised veil, Turkish out-door costume is absolutely hideous.

A large loose cloak called a "feredje" is thrown over the in-door dress, and this is so long that it has to be gathered up in front when the wearer walks, thus giving her the appearance of a moving bag or bundle. The huge, unshapely yellow boots also give a very ungainly appearance. Some of the fashionable ladies, however, are discarding these ugly over-alls, and are adopting French boots without heels.

Near the wall were drawn up "arabas" waiting for the ladies, and very magnificent "turn-outs" they were.

An araba is a native carriage that is much used by women, as it easily contains eight or ten persons. In shape it is something between a char-à-banc and a waggon, but is without springs. It is generally very gaily decorated and painted, and is comfortably cushioned inside. The top is covered with a thick red, green, or blue cloth that is fringed with gold. The white oxen that draw the carriages are generally beautiful creatures, and are also brilliantly adorned with red trappings and tassels, and have sometimes their foreheads painted bright pink or blue.

After a time our exhausted bodies became somewhat refreshed, and our crushed minds began to revive, and to face more courageously the duties of the day; so at last, summoning a strong resolution, we rushed across the hot court and over another burning "place," where the gravel felt as if it had been baked in an oven, and found ourselves in the Imperial armoury.

It was formerly an old chapel, and the remains of a great white marble cross at one end seemed to rebuke the desecration it is suffering.

There are some magnificent scimitars, made of the finest Damascus steel, and some of the hilts and scabbards are of gold, thickly encrusted with precious stones, but beyond these valuable decorations the collection of arms did not appear to be of much value. There are some hundreds of old matchlocks of an obsolete form, and probably of doubtful utility.

Amongst the curiosities are shown the Bells of Santa Sophia when it was a Christian church, the ancient keys of Constantinople, and the gorgeous scimitar of Sultan Mahmoud.

The Palace is but an assemblage of small buildings joined together by passages, and added to, from time to time, by successive sovereigns.

We passed through many large rooms or saloons, very handsome as to size, and richly ornamented with painting and gilding; but we thought them too low for their length, a defect that is increased by the heavy decorations of the ceilings.

There was but little furniture—only a few hard chairs besides the usual divan, and sometimes a console table with a French clock upon it.

Some of the smaller rooms were painted in arabesques, and had portières of blue or red satin over the doors.

From the position of the Palace, however, the views from the great recesses, full of windows, were quite enchanting.

A long low passage, hung with indifferent French and English prints, representing naval battles, storms at sea, &c., led to the bath-rooms—a pretty little set of apartments, with domed ceilings, beautifully fretted and painted.

The Sultan, however, has long ceased to reside here, and only comes on certain stated occasions, such as after the feast of the Bairam.

The grand procession from the mosque on that day is a magnificent pageant.

A crowd of court pages, resplendent with gold embroidery and brilliant dresses, precede the monarch, who, mounted on a matchless snow-white Arabian steed, rides slowly on, surrounded by all the great dignitaries of the Empire. The Pashas, habited in their state uniforms, are a mass of gold and precious stones, their saddles and the trappings of their horses being equally gorgeous.

Amidst all the magnificence of this group the Sultan alone is dressed with simplicity. He wears a dark frock coat with but little embroidery about it; but on the front of his fez and on the hilt of his sword blaze the enormous diamonds that are the pride of the Imperial treasury, while the housings of his Arab are almost hidden by the pearls and precious stones by which they are adorned.

On arriving at the Seraglio the Sultan proceeds to the throne-room, and there receives all his great officers of state. Ambassadors and foreign ministers are received at other times.

The Sultan goes in state to the mosque every Friday, and when he is then passing through the streets his people may approach him to present petitions.

The "temennah," as the ordinary mode of salutation is termed, is a very graceful gesticulation. The hand is bent towards the ground, as if to take up the hem of the superior's garment, and then pressed on the heart, forehead, and lips, to signify both humility and affection.

To call the pleasure-grounds that surround the Seraglio gardens, is a misnomer according to the European idea of what a garden should be, for there is scarcely a flower to be seen. They are a series of beautiful wildernesses, where the nightingales sing from the tangled thickets, and where each turn in the pathway, each opening amongst the trees, discloses some enchanting view, either of the bright blue Bosphorus, or of the misty grey of the distant mountains, or gives a peep of the city itself, whose innumerable domes and minarets rise dazzlingly white above the dark masses of cypress, their gilded crescents flashing brightly in the brilliant sunshine.

The soft rustling of the breeze amongst the trees, the sweet scent of the cypresses and flowering shrubs, all invited to a halt, and we seated ourselves on a piece of old wall, and idly watched the caïques as they glided across the Bosphorus.

Near us was a low gateway projecting over the sea, and in olden times its portals never opened, save when the sack was borne forth, that contained sometimes the living body of those odalisks whose conduct had not been *sans reproche*. In later years it is believed that these unhappy women were taken to a fortress called Roumel-Hissei, or Castles in Europe, and there strangled. Their bodies, sewn up in a sack, were then thrown into the middle of the stream, where the strength of the current would rapidly carry them out to sea. At any rate, whatever their punishment, the extent of it is never known beyond the walls of the Imperial Harem.

The flocks of little birds that are seen skimming so rapidly and so restlessly over the waves of the Bosphorus, are supposed by the Turks to be the souls of these unfortunates, who, for their great sin, are for ever condemned to seek in vain the lover who had led them astray.

CHAPTER III.
SECTS.

Although in olden times the Moslems were both cruel and fanatical in forcing their religion upon conquered nations, the Turks of to-day are exceedingly tolerant, and unlike the Mohammedans of Syria and Asia Minor, who abhor every denomination of Christians, permit Protestant, Roman Catholic, and Greek chapels to be erected without opposition in the neighbourhood of Constantinople.

Indeed, at this present time, the Sheyees, as the followers of Ali are called, are hated by the orthodox party, or Sünnees, far more intensely than any sects of Christians are.

However, notwithstanding the religious warfare that rages between the heads of these two great parties, almost every description of worship is tolerated by the Government, and there are as many Dissenters therefore in Constantinople as could be found in London. One of the most popular sects, especially amongst the lower classes, is that of the Dancing Dervishes, and it is a curious though a somewhat humiliating spectacle, to see by what extraordinary means men seek to do homage to their Creator.

The Dervishes assemble every Tuesday and Friday, the ceremonial being the same on both days. On arriving at the Tekké, or place of worship, we were taken to a large room on the upper storey. A gallery ran round three sides of this apartment, portions of it being partitioned off for the use of the Sultan and of Turkish ladies.

A large circular space is railed off in the centre of the room and reserved for the Dervishes. A few women and children, some Turkish officers and soldiers, were also seated in the gallery near us. No other foreigners were present besides ourselves.

About twenty Dervishes speedily arrived, and their Mollah or Sheik, a venerable old man, with a long white beard, seated himself before the niche that indicated the direction of Mecca. The Dervishes stood before him in a semicircle, without shoes, their arms crossed upon their breasts, and their eyes humbly cast upon the ground. They were all without exception pallid and haggard, and apparently belonged to quite the lower classes. One was a mere boy of about thirteen or fourteen, another was blind, a third was a negro.

After a few sentences, recited from the Koran, the Dervishes, headed by their mollah, began to march slowly round and round the enclosure, adapting their steps to the music (if it could be so called) of a tom-tom and a sort of flute, that from time to time uttered a low melancholy wail.

After having made four or five rounds, the mollah returned to his seat, and the Dervishes, throwing off their cloaks, appeared in white jackets and long yellow petticoats.

The mollah began to pray aloud, and, as if inspired by the prayer to which they listened with upturned faces, the Dervishes began to turn round; slowly at first, but then as the heavenly visions became more and more vivid, they extended their arms above their heads, they closed their eyes, and their countenances showed that they were in a trance of ecstatic joy.

The mollah ceased to pray, but round and round went the whirling figures, faster and faster. It was a wonderful sight, so many men moving with such rapidity, all apparently unconscious, yet never did one touch the other.

The only sound heard was the occasional flutter of a petticoat, and the unearthly noise of the music from the gallery, for as the movements became more rapid, so did the tom-tom increase in vehemence, and the wailings of the flute became more and more dismally dreadful.

The effect was singular upon us spectators in the gallery. After a time many of our neighbours seemed to become, as it were, infected with the extraordinary scene below, their eyes became fixed, and they began rocking themselves to and fro in rhythm with the movements of the Dervishes.

We were also becoming quite giddy from assisting at such a fatiguing religion, when, happily for us, the mollah bowed his head; in an instant each man stopped short, and bowed as quietly as if nothing had happened.

A few prayers and some sentences from the Koran were again recited, and the Dervishes, who were in a state of heat and exhaustion quite distressing to see, resumed their cloaks. They then knelt while more prayers were said. Each man then kissed the hand of the sheik and those of his brother Dervishes. A blessing was pronounced, to which the Dervishes responded by a cry, or rather howl, of Allah-il-Allah, and the ceremony was over. Having seen it, we no longer wondered at the pallid worn-out appearance of the worshippers, for the exhaustion both of mind and body must be very great. The object of the whirling is to distract the mind from earthly things, so as to enable the worshipper to concentrate himself upon the inexpressible joys of Paradise.

The exhibition, however, on the whole was painful. It is always sad to see Our Heavenly Father worshipped in a degrading manner by His children.

The Dancing Dervishes are said to be popular. They mostly lead blameless, inoffensive lives, and are very charitable.

Although the ceremonies of the Howling Dervishes have been much modified, and though many of the revolting cruelties they inflicted upon themselves have been suppressed by law, still the hideous howls and frantic actions to which they yield, as the inspiration possesses them, make their mode of worship a scene at which no woman can properly assist.

Passing one day in a caïque by a Tekké where the service of Howling Dervishes was going on, we were arrested by the most tremendous and savage yell that imagination can picture. So hideous and prolonged was the howl, that it seemed as if it must have come from a menagerie of wild beasts rather than from the throats of human beings.

These miserable fanatics begin their worship by placing their arms on each other's shoulders, they then draw back a step, and advancing suddenly, each man with a tremendous and savage yell howls forth, "Allah-Allah-Allah-hoo!" which must be repeated a thousand times uninterruptedly. Their countenances become livid, the foam flies from their lips, many of them fall on the floor in strong convulsions, from which they only rise to inflict cruel and horrid tortures upon their own wretched bodies.

The stream that runs through the Bosphorus from the Black Sea to the Sea of Marmora is so strong that it is almost impossible for a vessel to stem the current unless aided by steam. We thankfully, therefore, accepted the kind offer of the captain of the English man-of-war to take us in tow up to Beyuk'dere, a village near the entrance of the Black Sea.

The yacht was made fast apparently to the frigate, and off we set, but such was the force of the stream that, at an awkward corner near Bebek, the immense hawser, that looked as if nothing could break it, snapped in two like a bit of thread, and the yacht spun round with the velocity of an opera-dancer. Happily the danger had been foreseen and guarded against, but we were swept so close in against the shore that the jib-boom knocked down a piece of garden railing, and nearly spitted a most respectable old Turk, who was sitting calmly smoking on his terrace. Some time and much patience were required before the yacht could be again attached to the frigate, but at last two hawsers made her fast, and we proceeded on our way up the Bosphorus.

This beautiful stream is very unique in its characteristics, for while the waters have the depth, brilliancy, and life of the sea, its shores are cultivated and wooded like the banks of a river. The gentle sloping hills are covered with dwelling-houses and kiosks, while the terraces and gardens of stately palaces line the shore. The Turks have much taste, and are also great lovers of flowers. The gardens, therefore, are well laid out, and generally well kept. The climate also is favourable, though the winters are cold, snow sometimes lying on the ground for many days. The beautiful American trumpet-creeper grows in perfection, and may be seen hanging over almost every garden wall, its large bunches of orange-coloured flowers being in lovely contrast with the brilliant green foliage. Orange trees and myrtles do well, although they do not attain the same size and luxuriance as in Sicily and Greece.

Turkish houses are exceedingly picturesque in appearance. They are seldom more than two storeys high, have many irregular projections, and the overhanging roofs extend considerably beyond the walls. They are usually built of wood, and are painted white, stone colour, or pale yellow.

Both inside and out they look exquisitely clean; indeed, inside not a speck of dust is to be seen, the floors are covered with beautiful matting, and the walls are usually painted a delicate cream colour. But, alas! a Turkish house is but a whited sepulchre, for beneath this pure surface vermin prevail to such an extent that at night they come out by hundreds. It is a horrible plague, but by constantly painting and the free use of turpentine, most foreigners succeed in time in ridding their houses of these torments.

We once made a painful experience of the deceptiveness of appearances. During the summer, our evil angel induced us, and the Countess S——, the wife of one of the diplomats, to accept an invitation from a very rich Armenian merchant to assist at the marriage of his daughter. The fêtes were as usual to extend over three days, and we were to be his guests for that period.

The house was magnificent in size, and gorgeously decorated with gold, and velvet, and satin. The dinner, or supper, also was as grand as French and Turkish culinary art could make it. Our entertainers were kind and agreeable people, so we looked forward to a very pleasant visit.

We three Frank ladies had assigned to us as a sleeping apartment an immense saloon, superbly gilt and painted, but having little furniture besides a crimson satin divan, trimmed with gold fringe, that ran round three sides of the room. Adjoining was a small bath-room, and our maids had a room at some distance in another wing of the house.

On retiring to our apartment at night, we found three comfortable-looking beds had been prepared for us in the usual Eastern fashion—that is, laid on the floor.

Each bed had two thick soft mattresses, covered with pale green satin; the pillows were of the same rich material, and covered with cambric; the sheets were also of cambric, beautifully fine and white, and trimmed with broad lace. The coverlets were of green satin, embroidered, and fringed with gold.

Altogether our couches looked very inviting, especially after a long afternoon of civilities, and talk, besides the great dinner, and the long wedding ceremony, which did not take place till midnight.

The lights were put out, and we had just sunk into the pleasant half-conscious dreaminess of a first sleep, when we were thoroughly awakened by a sudden pattering and rush of little feet behind the walls, around, above, and below us, while sundry sharp squeaks announced the neighbourhood of rats.

However, travellers do not allow their night's rest to be disturbed for trifles; so, covering up our heads, in order to shut out the disagreeable noise, we resolved not to hear, and tried to go to sleep.

But it would not do; an unendurably loud squeal close to Madame S.'s head made her jump up hastily, thinking the rats must be in the room.

We lighted the candles, and then—our feelings can better be imagined than described, when we beheld an invading army of horrors worse than rats, descending the walls, marching over the floor, and creeping out of every little crack and hollow in the woodwork.

In blank dismay we looked at each other. What was to be done? The divans and ottomans had already been taken possession of by the enemy. There was not a cane chair or a table in the room, or we would have mounted upon them.

Help was impossible; there were no bells, we did not feel justified in disturbing the household, and we were ignorant of the whereabouts of our maids' room.

We were in despair, when a sudden bright inspiration flashed into the mind of one of us. The bath, the clean white marble, seemed to offer a safe refuge. In an instant we were there, and wrapping ourselves up as well as we could, there we remained till morning. Luckily for us it was a warm summer's night, or we should have caught our deaths of cold, for we were so eager to escape from our hateful enemies that we should have accepted any risk.

There we sat in forlorn discomfort—melancholy warning of the usual end of a party of pleasure. Luckily a sense of the ludicrousness of our position made us merry, for as each caught sight of the other's dismayed white face, we could not help bursting into fits of laughter, especially when we thought what our friends would have said could they have seen us.

When day came the foe retired; but as speedily as ordinary civility would permit, we took our leave, obliged to pretend important business in Constantinople, and resisting all the kind pressing of our host and his family, for nothing would have induced us to pass another night in such a chamber of horrors.

Our poor maids had slept, but showed lamentable traces of the presence of the foe, who evince decided partiality for fresh and newly-arrived foreigners.

An Armenian wedding has many forms that are akin to those of both the Turkish and Christian services. The ceremony is performed at midnight. The bride is so muffled up in shawls, and veils, and flowing garments, that face and figure are alike invisible. The fair damsel is not seen, but the mass of superb silk, lace, and flashing jewels placed in the middle of the room, indicate her presence. The bridegroom is asked, as he stands opposite to her, "Will you take this girl to be your wife, even if she be lame, deaf, deformed, or blind?" to which, with admirable courage and resignation, he replies, "I will take her." The officiating priest then joins their hands, a silk cord is tied round the head of each, and, after many prayers and much singing, they are pronounced man and wife.

CHAPTER IV.
THE HAREM.

The first visit to a Harem is a very exhausting business, for everyone feels shy, and everyone is stupid, and the stupidity and shyness last many hours.

We were fortunate, however, in paying our first ceremonious visit to the Harem of R—— Pasha, whose wife enjoys, and deservedly, the reputation of being as kind in manner as she is in heart. Madame P. was so good as to go with us as interpreter. We were afterwards accompanied by a nice old Armenian woman, well known amongst the Turkish ladies, as she attends many of them in their confinements, and is always summoned to assist at weddings and other festivals, besides being often trusted as the confidential agent for making the first overtures in arranging marriages.

Turkish babies have a hard time of it during the first month of their existence. Soon after their birth they are rubbed down with salt, and tightly swaddled in the Italian fashion. The pressure of these bandages is often so great that the circulation becomes impeded, and incisions and scarifications are then made on the hands, feet, and spine, to let out what Turkish doctors and nurses call "the bad blood." The unhappy little creature is only occasionally released from its bonds, and never thoroughly washed until the sacred month of thirty days has expired, when it is taken with its mother to the bath. No wonder that the sickly and ailing sink under such treatment, and that the mortality amongst infants should be frightful.

Scarcely had our caïque touched the terrace that extends before R—— Pasha's handsome palace, when a small door, that was hardly noticed in the long line of blank wall, opened as if by magic. We passed through, and found ourselves in a small shady court surrounded by arcades, up the columns of which climbing plants were trained. In the centre was a fountain, with orange trees and masses of flowers arranged around its basin. A broad flight of steps at the end of the court led to the principal apartments.

We were received at the foot of the stairs by two black slaves and several young girls dressed in white, who escorted us to a large saloon on the upper floor. The ceiling of this room was quite magnificent, so richly was it painted and gilt. There was the usual divan, and the floor was covered with delicate matting, but there was no other furniture of any sort.

The walls were exceedingly pretty, being painted cream colour, and bordered with Turkish sentences, laid on in mat or dead gold, a mode of decoration both novel and graceful. We learnt afterwards that many of the phrases were extracts from the Koran; others set forth the name and titles of the hanoum's father, who had been a minister of much influence and importance.

The windows were closely latticed, but notwithstanding the jealous bars, the views over the Bosphorus and the opposite shore of Asia were enchanting.

Here we were met by H—— Bey, the Pasha's eldest son, a good-looking boy, about eleven or twelve years of age, also dressed in white, but wearing some magnificent jewels in his fez, and by him conducted to another and smaller apartment, somewhat more furnished than the first, as it had a console table, with the usual clock, a piano, and some stiff hard chairs ranged against the walls.

As we entered the room, the folding-doors opposite were thrown open, and the hanoum (lady of the house), accompanied by her daughter, and attended by a train of women, advanced to meet us.

We had heard that this lady had once been a famous beauty. She was still of an age "à prétention," that is to say, about thirty-three or five, so we had pictured to ourselves something handsome, graceful, and dignified. We were stricken, therefore, almost dumb with surprise when we saw a woman, apparently nearer sixty than thirty, very short, and enormously fat, roll rather than walk into the room. Her awkward movements were probably as much caused by the extraordinary shape of her gown, as by her unusual size. Her dress, which is called an "enterree," and was but a slight and slender garment, was made of thin pink silk. It was open to the waist, very scanty in the skirt, and ended in three long tails, each about a yard wide, and which, passing on each side and between her feet, must have made walking quite a matter of difficulty.

This singular robe was fastened round the waist by a white scarf, and certainly did not embellish, nor even conceal the too great exuberance of figure.

To show that she received us as equals and friends, the hanoum wore no stockings, only slippers. When the mistress of the house enters in stockings it is a sign that she considers her visitors to be of inferior rank.

We thought the hanoum's head-dress as unbecoming as her gown. Her hair was combed down straight on each side of her face, and then cut off short; and she had a coloured gauze handkerchief tied round her head. The eyebrows were painted with antimony, about the width of a finger, from the nose to the roots of the hair, and the eyes were blackened all round the lids. Had the face, however, not been such an enormous size, it would have been handsome, for the eyes were large, black, and well shaped, and the complexion was fair and good; but the nose was too large, and the mouth was spoiled from there being no front teeth. However, she seemed a most good-tempered, kind, merry creature, and she nodded her head and smiled upon us, while uttering a thousand welcoming compliments, as if she were really glad to see her stranger guests.

The daughter was a nice-looking girl, about fourteen or fifteen, with a face that was more bright and intelligent than actually pretty. Her figure was slight and graceful, but nevertheless showed indications that in a few years she, like her mother, might become prematurely fat and faded.

The eyes were marvellously beautiful—so large and lustrous, that they seemed like lamps when the long black lashes were raised; but her mouth was quite spoiled by bad teeth, a singular defect in one so young. But Turkish women almost always lose their teeth early. They seldom use tooth-brushes, and are inordinately fond of sweetmeats, which they eat from morning till night.

The young lady also wore the "enterree," or tailed dress, which seemed to be a mark of distinction, for all the attendants wore short coats and full white trousers.

Mother and daughter were both dressed with studied simplicity, as Turkish ladies receive at home "en negligé." It is only when they pay visits that they array themselves sumptuously.

On the present occasion the slaves and women were gorgeously apparelled, and most magnificent was their attire—velvet, satin, cloth of gold, and precious stones quite dazzled the eye. It was in very earnest a scene from the "Arabian Nights."

When we had been duly placed on the divan, a young slave brought in a tray, on which were a bowl containing a compote of white grapes, another full of gold spoons, several glasses of iced water, &c.

Etiquette requires that a spoonful of the sweetmeat should be eaten, and the spoon then placed in the left-hand bowl. Some iced water is drunk, and then the tips of the fingers only should be delicately wiped with an embroidered napkin presented for the purpose.

A calm and graceful performance of this ceremony marks the "grande dame" amongst Turkish ladies, and many a foreigner has come to grief from being unacquainted with these little details.

In the story of Ivanhoe, Cedric the Saxon is described as having been despised by the Norman courtiers, because he wiped his hands with the napkin, instead of drying them in courtly fashion by waving them in the air; so likewise does a lady lose caste for ever in a Turkish Harem should she rub her *hands* with the napkin instead of daintily passing it over the tips of her fingers.

Now came more slaves bringing coffee. One carried a silver brazier, on which were smoking several small coffee-pots; another had the cups—lovely little things, made of exquisitely transparent china, and mounted on gold filigree stands; a third carried a round black velvet cloth, embroidered all over in silver. This is used to cover the cups as they are carried away empty.

Narghilés were now brought, and for some minutes we all solemnly puffed away in silence. For myself, personally, this was an anxious moment, for I very much doubted whether my powers as a smoker would enable me to undertake a narghilé, very few whiffs being often enough to make a neophyte faint. I looked at my sister; she was calmly smoking with the serenity and gravity of a Turk. The hanoum's eyes were fixed on vacancy. She had evidently arrived at her fifth heaven at least. The pretty daughter was looking at me, but I did not dare look at her; so, as there was no escape, I boldly drew in a whiff. Things around looked rather indistinct; however, I mustered up my courage and drew in another. It was not as disagreeable as the first, but the indistinct things seemed to get even fainter, and were, besides, becoming a little black, so I took the hint, and, finding nature had not intended me for a smoker, quietly let my pipe go out. Narghilés are now seldom used in harems except for occasions of ceremony. On all subsequent visits cigarettes were brought, which were much more easily managed.

When the pipes were finished we began to talk, and mutually inquired the names and ages of our respective children. The hanoum has three—the eldest son, H—— Bey, the daughter named Nadèje, and a little fellow about five years old, who came running in very grandly dressed, and with a great aigrette of diamonds in his little fez—evidently mamma's pet.

H—— Bey wanted very much to talk. But, alas! our Turkish words were sadly few, and conversation through an interpreter soon languishes and becomes irksome. We asked him his age, but he did not know. No Turk ever troubles himself or herself about so trivial a matter. They are satisfied to exist, and think it quite immaterial how many years they may have been in the world.

Amongst the attendants were two very old women, so dried up and so withered that they scarcely looked like women. One of them, who was blind, had been nurse to the hanoum. It was quite charming to see the kindness and tenderness with which these poor old creatures were treated. The blind nurse was carefully placed in a comfortable corner near the windows. H—— Bey constantly went to her, and from time to time, affectionately putting his arm round her neck, seemed to be describing the visitors to her. These old women were the only persons who were allowed to sit in the hanoum's presence; all the others remained standing in a respectful attitude, their arms crossed, and generally so motionless that they might have been statues but for the restless movement of their eyes.

Remembering the piano, we asked Nadèje if she liked music, and after some persuasion she played some wild Turkish airs with considerable facility and expression.

We were then invited to see the house, which was large and very handsome. Strangers are always at first, however, somewhat bewildered by finding there are no bedrooms; but, in fact, every room is a bedroom, according to necessity or the season.

Hospitality is almost a religious duty amongst the Turks, and every room is surrounded by cupboards, in which are stowed away vast numbers of mattresses and pillows ready for any chance guest who may arrive.

The mattresses are thick and comfortable, and are generally covered with some pale-coloured satin or silk. The beds are made upon the floor, and, besides the mattresses and pillows, have cambric or fine linen sheets and a silk coverlet.

Excepting the bathing apartments attached to the house, no appliances for washing were to be seen anywhere; and these ladies seemed surprised that we considered daily ablution necessary. They assured us that the bath twice a week was quite as much as was good for the health. Daily washing they consider a work of supererogation, so they satisfy themselves with pouring a little rose-water from time to time over their hands and faces.

Upon our expressing a wish to know how the "yashmak," or veil, was arranged, Nadèje immediately had one put on, to show how it ought to be folded and pinned; and as by this time we had become great friends, it was good-naturedly proposed that we should try the effects of yashmak and "feredje," and the most beautiful dresses were brought, in which we were to be arrayed.

Further acquaintance with the yashmak increases our admiration for it. The filmy delicacy of the muslin makes it like a vapour, and the exquisite softness of its texture causes it to fall into the most graceful folds.

Some of the feredjes, or cloaks, were magnificent garments. One was made of the richest purple satin, with a broad border of embroidered flowers; another of brocade, so thick that it stood alone; another of blue satin worked with seed pearls.

The jackets, "enterrees," &c. &c., were brought in piled upon trays and in numbers that seemed countless. A Parisian's wardrobe would be as nothing compared with the multitude and magnificence of the toilettes spread before us.

The jewels were then exhibited. Turkish jewellers generally mount their stones too heavily, and the cutting is far inferior to that of Amsterdam; but the hanoum had some very fine diamonds, really well set. One aigrette for the hair was exceedingly beautiful. The diamonds were mounted as a bunch of guelder-roses, each rose trembling on its stem. We also much admired a circlet of lilies and butterflies, the antennæ of the butterflies ending in a brilliant of the finest water. There was also a charming ornament for the waist, an immense clasp, made of branches of roses in diamonds, surrounded with wreaths of leaves in pearls and emeralds, a large pear-shaped pearl hanging from each point.

Having inspected the house we paid a visit to the garden, now as full of roses as an eastern garden should be. Terraces made shady by trellises of vines and fig-trees hung over the Bosphorus, and to every pretty view the falling waters of streams and fountains added their pleasant music to aid the soothing influence of the scene. At the end of one terrace was a large conservatory full of beautiful climbing plants; but we were afraid of admiring too much, for H—— Bey had accompanied us, and, after the manner of eastern tales, whenever we praised anything insisted upon giving it to us.

We were now preparing to take leave, but our friend's hospitality was not yet exhausted; and the hanoum, taking my sister and myself each by the hand, led us into the smaller saloon, where a collation had been prepared.

On a low circular table, or stool, a large tray had been placed, on which were a number of dishes containing melons, grapes, peaches, vegetable marrows, thin slices of cheese, and a variety of sweetmeats. Piles of bread cut into slices were also arranged round the tray. There were forks, but the bread supplied the place of spoons.

When we were all seated, rice, pillau, and little birds roasted in vine leaves were brought in, *à la Française*. The kabobs and maccaroni had too much garlic in them for our taste, but a very light sort of pastry called "paklava" was excellent, and the rice was perfection. The cooking we thought very good, and a great contrast to an experiment we had made a few days previously, in order to see what ordinary Turkish cookery was like.

One day during our many expeditions for sight-seeing in Constantinople, we were seized by the pangs of hunger several hours before we had arranged to return to Therapia, so espying a very nice clean-looking cook-shop, where a number of cooks, neatly dressed in white, were chopping and frying little scraps of meat, we proceeded there and ordered a dish of kabobs *à la Turque*. The kabobs in themselves might have been good, and also the fried bread that accompanied them, but a sauce of fat and garlic had been poured over both that made the dish not only uneatable, but unendurable. The good-natured cook seemed surprised at our bad taste, but yielded to European prejudices, and at last brought some plain rice and tomatoes, with which we made an excellent luncheon. The favourite Turkish sweetmeat, called "Rahat-la-Koum," or Lumps of Delight, is excellent when quite fresh, and makes much better *eau sucrée* than plain sugar, as there is a slight flavour of orange-peel and roses given to the water.

To return, however, to our little breakfast at R—— Pasha's; between each course of meat every one took what pleased her from the dishes on the table—fruits, sweetmeats, or cheese, though the latter was the favourite, as it is supposed not only to increase the appetite, but to improve the taste.

Both before and after eating, gold basins and ewers were brought round, and as we held our hands over the former perfumed water was poured upon them. The napkins were so beautifully embroidered in gold thread and coloured silks that it seemed quite a pity to use them for drying the hands. The repast over, coffee and cigarettes again appeared, and then, with many friendly invitations and kindly expressions, we parted.

The hanoum offers us her bath-room, her caïques, and her carriages, and proposes also to teach us Turkish.

In this harem, as is now generally the case in the best Turkish families, there is but one wife.

Our friend, the hanoum, had been a well-portioned bride. She brought her husband, besides the house we had seen, another at Beyuk'dere, considerable property in land, and a large sum of money. Where a daughter is so richly dowered, the father usually stipulates that no other wife shall be taken.

Wives also, in Constantinople, as elsewhere, are expensive luxuries, for each lady must have a separate establishment, besides retinue and carriages.

Marriage in Turkey is not a religious ceremony; it is merely a civil covenant that can be annulled for very trivial reasons by either party. Public opinion, however, pronounces such separations disgraceful, and they are seldom resorted to unless for grave reasons.

A man can put away his wife by pronouncing before a third person that his marriage is "void," but must in that case resign all the property that his wife has ever possessed. A woman can only obtain a divorce by going before a cadi, and declaring that she yields all her dower and property, and claims her freedom. Should there be children, the mother, if she so elects, can retain the girls with her until they are seven years old; after that age they return to their father's house, unless an especial arrangement has been made to the contrary.

A Turkish bath, when taken in a private house, is but a repetition of the ceremony that may be gone through in any of the principal bathing establishments in London and Paris; but public Turkish baths are quite national institutions, and often afford so many amusing and interesting scenes of real life that no foreigner should omit to visit them.

Wednesday is the day usually set apart for the Turkish women; Greek women have Saturday; the other days are allotted to the men.

The first time we went to the bath, we were quite oppressed with the extent of the preparations that our friends seemed to think absolutely necessary. Ladies are always attended by their own servants, and besides providing themselves with the necessary linen and toilet appendages, bring all the materials for the subsequent repast, with coffee and pipes.

Besides several dressing-gowns, there was quite a mountain of towels, so large that they might almost be called sheets; some of them long and narrow for wrapping round the head and drying the hair. There were wonderful-looking yellow gloves, of various degrees of coarseness, for rubbing. As we looked at them we quite shuddered at the thought of what we should have to endure. Then there were tall wooden clogs, to enable us to walk across the heated floors; and bowls of metal for pouring boiling water upon us. Besides these and many other implements apparently for torture, there were brushes and combs, various sorts of soap for washing, for rubbing, and for perfuming; bottles of scented waters, rugs, mattresses, looking-glasses; and, in addition to the basket containing cups, plates, and dishes, with all the paraphernalia for luncheon, there was a large box full of perfumes.

Perfumes in the East are not only countless in number, but of a strength almost overpowering to Western nerves. Literally, not only every flower, but every fruit, is pressed into the service of the perfumer.

First in rank and potency is the far-famed attar-gûl, of which one pure drop suffices to scent for years the stuff on which it is poured. The fine aromatic perfume of the orange and cinnamon flowers is well known, and the more delicate fragrance of the violet is preserved with all its fresh charm. Still, a box of Turkish perfumes is almost overpowering from its excess of sweetness; and, with the exception of the violets, we preferred the bottles unopened.

When, in addition to the articles already enumerated, we add that an extensive wardrobe was taken by each lady, that there were baskets of fruit, cases of confectionery, a complete coffee equipage, and all necessary appliances for smoking, it will easily be imagined that the "impedimenta," as the Romans so aptly called travelling luggage, was by no means small. To our uninitiated eyes it appeared truly formidable, but our friends seemed to think it all "en règle;" so we held our tongues and profited by the kind arrangements so affectionately made for us.

On arriving at the bath we passed through a narrow passage and came to a large vaulted room, with a double balcony round two sides of it. The lower balcony, which was about two or three feet from the ground, was divided by curtains into compartments. These compartments were occupied by ladies either preparing for or reposing after the fatigues of the bath. In the latter case the curtains were drawn back, and the inmate could be seen reclining in indolent enjoyment upon her satin mattress. Occasionally she would raise the cup of coffee or sherbet to her lips, or, with closed eyes, would languidly smoke the scented cigarette as her maid combed her hair, or tinged the delicate tips of her fingers with the beautifying henna.

Some of the recesses disclosed less gratifying spectacles. Here an ancient dame, whom the bath had restored to her natural state of white hair and wrinkles, was having the renovating process performed of having her scanty locks dyed red, and the hollows and furrows that time had made filled up by white paint and rouge.

The passion of Turkish women for cosmetics is almost unaccountable, for the complexions of most of them are exceedingly good. Their skins are generally of a creamy white, with a delicate shade of colour; but nothing will satisfy them but the most startling contrast of white and pink, and it is pitiable to see quite young girls so disfigure themselves.

It required a little effort of courage, when fully arrayed in the long white bathing-gown and mounted on the tall pattens, to issue forth from our recess; but we pushed aside the curtains and appeared, feeling very much, as we essayed to walk on the slippery marble floor, as an unhappy cat must do who, with walnut shells on her feet, is forced to perform a promenade on the ice. Two ancient bath-women speedily came to our assistance. They had been slowly boiling so many years that they were shrivelled and parched out of the semblance even of "wo-manity," if such a word may be permitted. Strange to say they had but few wrinkles, but their skin seemed tightly drawn over their faces, as over the bones of a skull, and hung loosely in great folds under their chins and around their throats. They told us afterwards that they had been attendants to the bath for upwards of thirty years, and had grown so much accustomed to the heated and sulphureous atmosphere in which they pass the greater portion of their days, that a purer and fresher air is quite painful to them. By their aid, with much trepidation, we stumbled across the hall, and in a few seconds found ourselves in a sort of pandemonium next door. In an instant I felt as a shrimp, if he feels at all, must feel in hot water—I was boiled. I looked at my companion; her face was a gorgeous scarlet. In our best Turkish, and with faint and imploring accents, we gasped out, "Take us away!" All in vain. For those who enter here there is no retreat—

"Lasciate ogni speranza voi ch'entrate."

We had come to be boiled and rubbed, and boiled and rubbed we must be.

We speedily found ourselves seated close to a small stream of what, at first, seemed like boiling water, of which large bowlfuls were rapidly thrown over us. When we had a little recovered from this shock, and our eyes became more accustomed to the clouds of sulphureous vapours that were rolling around, we began to look with interest on the singular scene in which we found ourselves.

There were upwards of a hundred women in the bath, the bathers seated in groups of two or three by each little stream of hot water. Each woman was attended by one or two slaves, who were assiduously rubbing their mistress with perfumed soap, or pouring the steaming bowls of boiling water over her.

Numbers of children, without an atom of clothing upon them, were running about shouting, laughing, and throwing water upon each other. Many babies also were having a bath against their will, and the shrieks of these unfortunates were quite deafening. Most of the women were talking and laughing, and the great height of the hall caused a reverberation that made the noise most bewildering. The dense atmosphere and rolling clouds of steam made it also impossible to ascertain the size of the bath, which however must have been very large, from the number of persons it contained. From it opened numerous small rooms still hotter than the first, although the shock on entering was not nearly as great as that experienced when arriving at the great hall. Here the soaping and rubbing processes were performed with such vigour that we felt as if nothing was left of us, and right glad were we when we found ourselves once more in the comfortable dressing-room, with just enough strength left to throw ourselves on the luxurious mattresses and appreciate, to its full extent, the kindness that had supplied us with coffee, fruit, luncheon, &c. How many hours passed in pleasant idleness, it is impossible to say. One takes no note of time after a Turkish bath; and also, when a little refreshed and revived, we were exceedingly amused and interested by the scenes and conversations around us.

It seemed that those who wished to have a private dressing-room, such as that we had, paid a little more than the ordinary price, the majority of the ladies availing themselves of the large general dressing-rooms on the balcony above.

Towards the afternoon the bathing was almost over, and the club, as it were, began. The whole of the immense space below us was occupied by groups of ladies, who, reclining on their mattresses, chattered to each other, smoked, drank coffee, and ate fruit, as their maids dried, combed, and dyed their hair, for there were but few who did not use a little henna. The children, who were now clothed, ran about as before, but happily most of the suffering babies had gone to sleep.

Two middle-aged ladies near us were evidently, and with much diplomacy, negotiating the preliminaries of a marriage. Contrary to the usual state of the case in Europe, the "riches" of the lady and the "beauty" of the gentleman were amply dilated upon.

A little further on two handsome young women, probably the inmates of the same harem, had evidently had a violent quarrel, only subdued by the soothing influence of the bath. Beyond them a fair Georgian, the prettiest woman in the room, reclined negligently against a heap of cushions; her slaves were deluging her with perfumes, while a hideous old crone was earnestly whispering some tale into her ear, probably one of love, as the girl coloured and looked pleased, as she occasionally glanced suspiciously around, as if to assure herself that no one was listening to the communication.

In one corner a group of matronly-looking women were describing the merits and charms of their respective babies, while shouts of merry laughter, proceeding from another, showed where a number of young girls had collected together. The whole scene was singularly picturesque and interesting, and gave us a very favourable impression of the native refinement of Turkish women.

Nothing could be more decorous than the appearance and manners of every woman there present, but in one respect we were disappointed. There was a remarkable want of beauty. With the exception of the pretty Georgian, there was scarcely a good-looking woman in the room. The handsomest were, beyond all question, some coal-black Nubian slaves. One of them had the most beautiful figure we had ever seen. Tall, lithe, and supple, her small head exquisitely poised on a throat round and shapely as that of a statue, she moved about with the undulating grace of some wild animal. Coal-black though she was, her features had none of the unseemly coarseness and grotesqueness of the negro; on the contrary, the nose was delicately cut, while her mouth, though full, had the waving lines of beauty, only seen in the Egyptian sphinx.

Although a Turkish bath is certainly a most inviting luxury, and has temporarily a flattering effect upon the skin, making it for some hours, even days afterwards, exquisitely white, smooth, and soft, still, owing to the great heat, and the quantity of sulphur with which the air is charged, an undue indulgence in bathing has in the end a deteriorating effect upon female beauty. The muscles become relaxed, and the skin, although it remains soft and delicate, loses its elasticity; the hair also rapidly falls off, and what is left becomes thin and weak. The too devoted votaries of the bath, therefore, speedily become enervated both in mind and body, and whilst still young in years fade into a premature old age. The indolence also which it creates does much to increase the tendency to undue corpulence, so destructive to the fair proportions of Eastern women. Most of them, after middle life, either become shrivelled and dried up, or else have both features and form swelled to very uncomely dimensions.

CHAPTER V.
THE HAPPY VALLEY.

Amongst the many lovely valleys that surround Constantinople, the two most perfectly charming are the Valley of the Sultan and that called by the Franks the Sweet Waters of Asia. Both are carpeted by the freshest and greenest sward; both are shaded by magnificent trees; and numerous little streams, descending from the neighbouring heights, not only charm by the pleasant music of their waters, but enable pleasure-seekers to boil their coffee *al fresco*.

These delicious spots, so green and fresh, nestled, as it were, amidst comparatively barren hills, seem to invite all the happy ones of earth to come and repose under the tender shade of their great trees. The air, though soft, is so fresh and invigorating, that the fact of existence seems a joy. Nature rejoices on all sides—the brilliant sky above, the bright rays glancing through the trees, the merry little wavelets that show their white heads upon the intense blue of the Bosphorus, the birds singing blithely from every coppice and tangled brake—all nature smiles in sunshine, hope, and joy. Little troubles and unworthy anxieties fade and fall away, and life seems for a few short hours to be the delight that Our Heavenly Father probably once meant it to be.

There are few things more charming in the Turkish character than the honest, hearty love for the beauties of nature that prevails in all classes. From the Sultan to the meanest and poorest of his subjects, whenever a holiday occurs, all hasten to enjoy the luxury of fresh air and the soft green sward, there to while away the few hours (perhaps in both cases) hardly wrung from many days of weary and exhausting toil. In the winter the men of course frequent the coffee-shops, there to enjoy their pipes and the long histories of the professional story-tellers, but in the summer every valley is thronged with people, all evidently enjoying themselves with a completeness and an absence of Western *ennui* that is most refreshing to behold.

Many a delightful hour did we pass in these valleys. The merry melodious voices of the women, the ringing laughter of the children, made a music very pleasant to the ear; and the eye was charmed with the brilliant beauty of the colouring, and the picturesque grace of the groups that surrounded one on every side.

On a Friday, or other holiday, many hundreds of people congregate at the Sweet Waters both of Europe and Asia. The women, arrayed in gorgeous dresses, recline on carpets beneath the trees, little spirals of smoke ascend from the numerous pipes, the narghilé bubbles in its rose-water, the tiny cups of coffee send forth a delicious fragrance, the perfume of fresh oranges and lemons fills the air. The still more exquisite sweetness of orange blossoms is wafted towards us, as a gipsy flower-girl passes through the groups, carrying many a mysterious bouquet, of which the flowers tell a perhaps too sweet and too dangerous love-tale to the fair receiver.

Then a bon-bon seller comes, laden with his box of pretty sweets. Many are really good, especially the sweetmeat called Rahat-la-Koum, when quite fresh, and another, made only of cream and sugar flavoured with orange-flower water.

Every now and then the wild notes of some Turkish music may be heard from the neighbouring hills—the band of a passing Turkish regiment; or perhaps the monotonous but musical chant of some Greek sailors falls on the ear, as they struggle to force their boat up the tremendous stream of the Bosphorus.

Seen from a little distance, and shaded by the flattering folds of the "yashmak," Oriental women almost always look pretty; but when, as they often do, the fair dames let the veil fall a little, and the features become distinctly visible, the illusion is lost at once.

The eyes are magnificent, almond-shaped, tender and melting, but, with very few exceptions, the nose and mouth are so large and ill-formed, that the face ceases to be beautiful; the superb eyes not compensating for the want of finish in the other features.

As a class, the Armenians were the best-looking, but the women's head-dress was remarkably becoming. They wear a thin coloured handkerchief, with a broad fringe of gauze flowers, tied coquettishly on one side of the head, long plaits of hair being arranged round it like a coronet.

As in Western countries, the middle and lower classes seemed to enjoy themselves the most. They sat on the grass, and talked to their friends. They could eat their fruit and drink their coffee *al fresco*, while some of the Sultan's odalisks, and other great ladies, shut up in their arabas and carriages, performed a slow and dreary promenade up and down the middle of the valley.

Very weary did some of these poor things look, but the guard of black slaves on each side the carriage forbade any hope of an hour's liberty. Happily, excepting in the Sultan's harem, it is now becoming the fashion for the ladies to descend from their carriages and to pass the afternoon beneath the trees.

Many other Eastern fashions are also becoming modified. The huge yellow boots are disappearing, French ones taking their place; parasols and fans are also used, and all the fashionable ladies now wear gloves.

Besides the charming valleys already mentioned, the shores of the Bosphorus abound in pretty villages, where the great Turkish families, the foreign ministers, and principal European merchants have palaces, and where they generally pass the summer.

The most important of these villages are Therapia and Beyuk'dere. The English and French ambassadors have each a palace at the former, and as we had the good fortune to pay a long and most happy visit to our kind friends at the English Embassy, we came to love Therapia as a very dear and happy home.

There is no place in the world, perhaps, where the air has so exhilarating an effect as on the shores of the Bosphorus. The soft, sweet breeze from the hill side seems to temper the fresh, salt wind that is borne in from the Black Sea; and how great was the delight when we sometimes turned to the sea-shore, after a long ride in the forest of Belgrade!

Can anything be more beautiful on a sunny evening than to watch the sea steal quietly up the glittering beach?—to see wave after wave gracefully bend its snow-capped head, and then, falling over, leave a line of shining water all along the shore? And riding down upon the cool, wet sand, how grateful to the tired horses is the tender lapping of the soft, soothing water, as the little waves curl round their heated feet! Ah! why will happy hours pass so soon away?—why does a pang ever mingle with the thought of a joy that is past?

Beyuk'dere is so pretty, so graceful, and so unreal-looking, especially as we saw it for the first time, on a bright moonlight night, that it seemed like a dream or a scene in a play. And yet the houses are very real, and some of them very handsome; for example, the Russian Embassy, where a clever and charming host, excellent dinners, and most agreeable evenings were very delightful realities.

Still, most of the smaller houses look as if they were cut out of cardboard. They have also an unusual number of windows, which, when lighted up at night (and the shutters are seldom closed, on account of the heat), give many of the streets the appearance of the side-scenes at the opera. So strong is the illusion, that it is difficult to cease expecting that the beautiful heroine in muslin apron, with little pockets, will presently look out of the latticed window, or that the irascible father, in brown coat and large buttons, will issue forth from that most fragile and operatic-looking door.

When we had been a few weeks at Constantinople, and had visited some half-dozen harems, we began to think we knew something about Turkish life, and it was not until we had been there some months, and become acquainted with the families of most of the principal pashas, ministers, &c., that we discovered how little we really knew about it.

But although we might change our opinions respecting many domestic customs and manners, time and more intimate knowledge of their character only increased our liking and admiration for the Turks, both men and women.

Benevolence and kindness are the principal characteristics of both sexes. During the whole period of our stay in Turkey we never saw even a child ill-treat a hapless animal.

Travellers, especially women, are seldom sufficiently conversant with the laws of a country to be able to expatiate with much accuracy on such matters. Turkish laws are said to be bad; perhaps they are so, but certainly there are few cities in Europe where the streets can be so safely traversed, both by night and day, as those of Constantinople.

Turkish manners, also, are peculiarly agreeable. Turks are not ashamed to show that they wish to please—that they wish to be courteous; happily they have not yet adopted that brusquerie of manner that is becoming so prevalent in the West.

The fault is perhaps an overabundance of ceremony and etiquette. Even in their own houses, in the seclusion of home, the master of a family is treated with a respectful deference which would astonish many Christian sons, who unhappily often now only look upon their father as the purse-holder, out of whom they must wring as much money as possible.

In the Selamluk1 no person seats himself without the permission of the master of the house; in the harem the same etiquette is observed, the hanoum, or first wife, reigning there supreme.

We had often heard that Eastern women enjoyed in reality far more liberty than their Western sisters, and in some respects this is certainly true; but in point of fact the liberty they possess in being able to go in and out unquestioned, to receive and pay visits where they choose, does not at all compensate for the slavery of the mind which they have to endure, from being cut off from the education and mental improvement they would gain by association with the other sex.

Mental imprisonment is worse even than bodily imprisonment, and by depriving a woman of legitimate ambition, by taking from her the wish for mental culture, she is reduced to the condition of a child—a very charming one, probably, when young, but a painful position for her when, youth having departed, the power of fascination decays with the loss of beauty; and though in some instances it is well known that the natural talent of the woman has had the power of retaining her husband's heart, still it too often happens that, after very few years of love and admiration, he turns to one still younger and fairer to charm his hours of leisure.

Not only did we constantly see Madame R—— and her charming daughter Nadèje, and the wives and relatives of the ministers, &c., whose acquaintance we made, but we had the honour of being invited to pay visits to most of the members of the imperial family; and the more we saw of the Turkish ladies the more we liked the kindly, gentle-hearted women who received us with such friendly hospitality.

In the royal palaces there was of course more splendour, more gold, more diamonds, more slaves—especially the hideous black spectres, who are often so revoltingly frightful that they look like nightmares. But in all essentials a description of a visit to one harem serves to describe the receptions at all.

During our visits to their wives the pashas often requested permission to enter the harem, and we were delighted to make the acquaintance of F—— Pasha, a statesman distinguished throughout Europe by his enlightened views, his generous nature, and by the improvements his wise legislation has effected for his country. Successive visits, both to his lovely palace on the Bosphorus and to us on board the yacht, turned this acquaintance into a friendship which we valued as it indeed deserved.

It was sometimes amusing to see the astonishment of the women when they found we did not object to converse with the pasha. They could hardly understand that we would allow him to enter the harem during our stay there.

In deference to their feelings we, however, always drew down our veils before the master of the house entered, a proceeding which we were aware materially increased their respect for us, and for our sentiments of reserve and propriety.

More intimate acquaintance with our Turkish friends enabled us to see how often they were annoyed and disturbed, probably quite unintentionally, by the proceedings of their European guests.

Madame F—— is a charming person, clever and intelligent to an unusual degree. She is said to possess great and legitimate influence with her husband. She invited us one day to a large party, consisting of most of the "lionnes" of the Constantinopolitan world.

Some of these ladies were very pretty, and perhaps rather fast. Many of them had adopted several French fashions, wearing zouaves and Paris-cut bodies instead of their own pretty jackets and chemises, a change we thought much for the worse. The great mixture of colours, also, which looks so well in the Turkish full dress of ceremony, seemed much out of place in a semi-French costume.

Our Paris bonnets produced quite a furore. So much were they admired that we lent them to be tried on by the whole assembly. Each fair Turk thought she looked lovely in the ludicrous little fabric of lace and flowers, though we would not be so untruthful as to say they were half as becoming as their own fez, with the grand aigrettes of diamonds, which they place so coquettishly on the side of their pretty heads.

These ladies were wonderfully "well up" in all the gossip of Constantinople. They were perfectly cognisant of all the little details of every embassy and legation, knowing every member of them by sight.

They have a game which is played for sugarplums. Various diplomats or well-known persons are imitated by some peculiarity they have, such as a mode of walking, talking, bowing, &c. The spectators have to guess who is meant, every failure being paid for by a certain number of bon-bons.

Of course the descriptions are unflattering; the more they are so the greater being the laughter excited. Many of the described would have been astonished could they have seen how cleverly they were caricatured. There was a luckless secretary of one of the smaller legations who seemed a favourite victim, as he certainly had many "odd" ways.

Amongst the many distinguished men whose acquaintance we made was C—— Pasha, a man who in talent may perhaps rival, but who in moral qualities is far below, F—— Pasha. In fact, C—— Pasha, from the stormy impetuosity of his character, and from an unfortunate tendency he has of occasionally taking the law into his own hands, rather resembles the old Turk as he was, than the modern Turk as he is.

C—— Pasha is a handsome man, about fifty years of age, with a very intellectual, acute face. A singularly square chin, and a closely-compressed mouth, give an expression of fierce determination, almost amounting to cruelty, to the countenance when in repose. As soon as he speaks, however, the whole face lights up with a kind of merry good-humour, which is inexpressibly winning; and though, if all tales may be believed, he is somewhat of a Bluebeard, and has committed crimes which, in other countries, would have brought him to the scaffold, it is impossible not to be pleased, almost in spite of oneself, by a manner unusually frank and earnest.

There is a story (let us hope it is only a story, and not a truth) that he put to death, with his own hand, one of his odalisks, and a young secretary to whom he had seemed much attached. It is said that the pasha, walking one day in his garden, saw a rose thrown from a window in the harem. The flower was picked up by the secretary, who put it to his lips, and kissed it passionately as he looked up at the lattice. Burning with indignation and jealousy, the pasha hastily repaired to the harem, and saw a young slave looking out of the window from which the rose had been thrown. Drawing his knife, he crept softly behind the unfortunate girl, and in an instant had plunged it into her throat. The death-cry of the unhappy victim startled the household, and the secretary, finding the intrigue had been discovered, at first fled to the hills, but subsequently took refuge with one of the foreign ministers. He remained in the latter's household for a considerable time—so long, indeed, that he flattered himself the affair had been forgotten.

At the expiration of some months, C—— Pasha sent or wrote to the young man, requesting him to return, and assuring him that, as he had thus with his own hand punished the guilty woman, his anger had been appeased.

The secretary, therefore, resumed his post, and for some weeks all apparently went well. One day, however, the pasha, attended by his secretary, was again walking in the garden. On arriving at the spot where the rose had fallen, the pasha requested the young man to gather a flower that was growing near. Unsuspicious of danger, the secretary obeyed, and as he bent down for the purpose, was stabbed to the heart by his revengeful master.

This deliberate murder—for such, in fact, it was—made a considerable stir for a time; but the high rank and great influence of the offender prevailed against justice, and the affair was ultimately hushed up, the pasha, it is believed, having only to pay a considerable sum of money to the family of the murdered man.

It must not be supposed that there are many, if indeed any, modern Turks like our agreeable but unprincipled friend; but it is said that occasionally an erring odalisk disappears, and as it is nobody's business to inquire about her, no troublesome questions are asked.

---

1 Apartments belonging to the men.

CHAPTER VI.
AN EASTERN BANQUET.

Shortly before our departure from Constantinople, we were so fortunate as to assist at a very grand Turkish breakfast. It was given by A—— Pasha in honour of the brother of the Viceroy, and to it were invited the principal members of the foreign embassies and legations, the Turkish ministers, Lord S——, and our humble selves.

The banquet was to take place in a lovely kiosk belonging to A—— Pasha, at Anokoi, a village on the Bosphorus, between Therapia and Pera.

As the English ambassador's state caïque passed the different military stations on its way down the Bosphorus, the drums beat, and the guard turned out to do honour to the great man; a proceeding far more agreeable to us spectators than to the *attaché*, who, having been "told off" for the purpose, was placed in a prominent part of the boat, that he might perpetually take off his hat in answer to the incessant salutes.

On arriving at Anokoi, we found the landing-place beautifully arranged with awnings, carpets, and flags. Gaily-decorated arabas also were in waiting to convey the guests to the top of the hill on which the kiosk stands.

The road was steep and dusty, and the day was hot, so that we were not sorry to arrive at our destination; but had the way been twice as steep, and even if we had had to ascend it on foot, it would have been worth the climb to see the magnificent view. The kiosk was built on the edge of a rocky but wooded bank hanging over the Bosphorus, and being thus on nearly the highest point near Constantinople, an exquisite panorama of sea and land was stretched before us, bounded only on one side by the lovely blue outline of Olympus, on the other by the expanse of misty grey that marked the Black Sea.

Our host, A—— Pasha, a specimen of the accomplished modern Turkish gentleman, met us at the entrance of the garden. Besides being very good-looking and agreeable, he speaks French admirably well, having been minister and ambassador at several foreign courts. This was, in fact, a farewell entertainment, as he was soon leaving Constantinople for the post to which he had just been nominated.

The banqueting-room was a large and lofty hall, beautifully painted in the Munich fashion, and handsomely furnished with satin hangings and curtains, abundantly supplied with Parisian couches, chairs, and lounges.

The table was adorned with a profusion of gold and silver plate, interspersed with groups of flowers very artistically arranged.

The *déjeûner* was excellent, but immensely long, for after the cinnamon, vegetable, white, and other soups, came an apparently endless procession of meats, boiled, baked, roasted, and stewed. There were whole animals and minced ones, also chickens and other poultry, stewed with pistachios and olives, fish rolled into balls and cooked with raisins, little birds wrapped in leaves, rice in many ways, pillau, caviare, fish known and unknown, innumerable vegetables and cheeses, and upwards of twenty sorts of sweets. The cookery was very good, though some of the dishes were overabundantly spiced for a Western palate.

The pastry was admirable, and the conserves quite the perfection of culinary art, for not only were the fruit and flowers excellent to eat, but they were beautiful to look at, the orange-flowers, rose-buds, and violets retaining their shape and colour as well as their flavour. The Armenians, who are the principal confectioners, jealously guard their most celebrated recipes, that descend in many families as precious heirlooms from father to son.

I was so fortunate as to be seated next a diplomat who thoroughly understands and appreciates both Turkish and French cookery in all their minutest branches. He was kind enough to superintend my dinner, and an admirable selection he made, though at the same time it must be confessed that he seasoned the "plats" by such brilliant conversation that the contents of the plate before me were often unnoticed.

To eat of such an army of dishes was impossible; some of the unlearned attempted it, not knowing, luckless creatures, what was before them, but broke down early in the day, and were "nowhere" when the fruit came. This was really a loss, for a murmur of admiration passed round the table, even the most trained and hardened old gourmands not being able to refrain from praise when the immense piles of fruit, in the perfection of their delicate beauty, were brought in—grapes, pines, peaches, apricots, figs, pomegranates, Japanese medlars, dates, almonds, nectarines, melons, citrons, oranges, sweet lemons—it is impossible to recollect even the names, but each fruit was so beautiful that an artist would have said it was a picture. However, its fair loveliness did not preserve it from being eaten, for Constantinople is a climate which makes fruit a necessary of life; without it one would really have fever.

There were two bands, one instrumental and one vocal, that performed alternately during breakfast. The voices in the latter were not bad, though rather nasal, but the pieces they sang were pitched too high, and in consequence sounded monotonous and strained. The instrumental music was infinitely better. There were some Wallachian gipsy airs which were perfectly charming. Wild and mournful, like most national music, they were full of character, and every now and then a tender melody broke forth that was inexpressibly touching.

A—— Pasha was so kind as to send us the next day the music of those we most admired, but without the wild, savage clang of Eastern instruments they lose much of their effect.

When the breakfast was at length over, we all adjourned to the garden, where sofas and chairs had been placed in the shade, round a small fountain.

Coffee and pipes were brought, and very merry and amusing was the talk.

Certainly the Ottomans are moving onwards with the times. A hundred years ago who would have supposed that a grave Turk would have been entertaining, not only Christians, but Christian women, and also devoting himself to them with an attention and kindness worthy of the most "preux chevalier" in Christendom?

Rich and luxurious as had been the entertainment, the arrival of the pipes formed the culminating point of magnificence.

Many of them were so encrusted with jewels that it was difficult to form any estimate as to their value. The pieces of amber of which they were made were almost priceless, both for their size and the delicacy of their tint. Yellow amber should be of the palest primrose hue, but there is another shade that is now much prized, namely, the black amber. This is exceedingly rare, and of course, therefore, exceedingly costly.

The pasha was kind enough to give us a piece when he paid his last farewell visit the day before we left the Bosphorus. Most of our kind friends came on board the yacht that day to wish us good-bye and God speed, for at dawn the next day we were to sail for the Crimea, and to judge by the stories that have been poured into our ears for some weeks past, the perils of the Black Sea for a sailing vessel must not only be very numerous, but very extraordinary.

Unluckily the only "*detaining*" result has been that our maid has taken fright, and resolutely refuses to leave Constantinople. She says that, though devotedly attached to us, she does not think it right to put herself to death for anybody, especially as she has an old mother dependent upon her. She proposes, however, to return to us should we come back alive, which with tears in her eyes she declares is "most improbable." Such being the cheerful view taken of our expedition, we find it impossible on such short notice to replace her. The few maids to be found here have an idea that we are doomed to death, and no amount of wages can tempt them to share our fate. One day we were buoyed up by the hope that there was a female heart stout enough to share our perils, but when a colossal German, about five feet ten high, and broad in proportion, appeared before us, *our* courage failed, and we felt she would be an incubus not to be endured. Besides, it would be a question of the nicest calculation whether, provided even if she could get down the companion, she could by possibility squeeze into her cabin. The idea, too, of getting her on deck, should there be any sea, made the brain lose itself in a maze of distressing conjectures.

As for ourselves, we began to grow proud of our courage in braving such unknown dangers, and felt rather like Christian in "Pilgrim's Progress," as he prepares to plunge into the flood, and penetrate the dark mist that veils the other side.

But in truth the opening into the Black Sea is often a very "uncanny" looking place, for at every change of weather a dense white fog hangs over it.

All the bad winds are said to come from the Black Sea, all the rain, all the squalls, so that at any rate, deserved or undeserved, it has got a very bad name, and we know that a bad name, whether given to a dog, a man, or a sea, loses nothing by time or telling.

The sea was calm, and the wind was favourable; but our first day's sail on the Black Sea was marked, and our hearts were troubled by a domestic calamity.

About ten days before we left the Bosphorus a bottle had been let down into the water to cool, and when it was drawn up again a curious little fish was found entangled in the string. It was about five inches long, and had the head of a horse, with the body and tail like those of the old fabulous dragon. We found it was called the Hippocampus, or Sea Horse; and though not uncommon on the coasts of Japan and China, it is rarely seen in these seas, and still more rarely taken alive.

The Russian Ambassador, Prince L——, who happened to be on board when the capture was made, is a great naturalist, and by his advice we put our prize into a glass bowl, with a small supply of its favourite seaweed. For many days the little creature did very well, and we used to watch with much interest its active, graceful movements. One morning, to our great astonishment, we found our friend surrounded by an immense family, about fifty little ones having made their appearance during the night. The mother seemed none the worse for such a prodigious event; and her children, who were about a quarter of an inch long, and perfect sea-horses in miniature, darted about with as much activity and liveliness as their parent.

We were so unfortunate as to possess an excellent steward,—Domenico by name, Neapolitan by birth,—who, with the most earnest endeavours to do right, and with the most anxious activity in so doing, always contrived to understand everything *à travers*, and who, therefore, by his misplaced zeal and energy, often drove us to the verge of distraction by his well-intentioned but unlucky efforts. We had, of course, given him strict orders never to touch our little pets.

The yacht lay-to just opposite a small village at the entrance of the Black Sea, and here Domenico went on shore to get some of the necessaries always required at the last moment. Seeing some of the seaweed which we needed for our little fish, and which it was not always easy to get, he wisely brought back some with him, but in his unwise zeal was rashly putting it into the bowl when, being suddenly called, he turned hastily, and stumbled, upsetting the glass and its precious contents. The mother was put back alive, but alas! all the fragile little ones were dead. Great was our grief and vexation, and we had not even the consolation of scolding the wretched Domenico. He was so distressingly contrite and unhappy at the fatal results of his disobedience, that he left us nothing to add to the storm of reproaches that he showered upon himself. The mother sea-horse lived for about a fortnight after this sad misfortune; whether she mourned at having thus lost, at one fell swoop, all her large little family, or whether she herself had sustained some injury, we could never discover; but she dwindled and dwindled, and was found one day dead; so all we could do was to preserve her little remains in spirits of wine. We had given a great many of the young ones to Prince L——, who wished to take them to St. Petersburg with him, but they did not survive many days, and their little dried bodies alone reached their destination.

A favourable breeze soon carried us within sight of the coast of the Crimea. The air was balmy, the sea was bright, though it had no longer the intense blueness that is so characteristic of the Bosphorus and the Mediterranean; the atmosphere, also, had a certain mistiness about it more akin to northern regions. We were not very far from the land, and could see that the country was flat and barren. In the far distance we could trace the faint outlines of a range of hills.

CHAPTER VII.
EUPATORIA.

We coasted on, the shore becoming lower and lower, until at length nothing was to be seen but an arid, sandy plain stretching away for miles. Not a tree or house broke its dull uniformity.

In the midst of this gloomy desert is Eupatoria. It would be difficult to find a more wretched-looking little place. The town consists of a tumble-down mosque, a couple of Christian churches, a caravanserai for strangers, and a few low miserable houses. There is also a small wooden landing-place, and a few huts, like sentry-boxes, scattered along the shore.

These huts, however, make the fortune, such as it is, of Eupatoria. They are the famous mud baths well known in the Crimea, and during the summer are resorted to, from all parts of Southern Russia, by persons afflicted with skin diseases.

There is one sad malady for which these baths are peculiarly efficacious. This complaint consists in the skin becoming so thin that at times the slightest exertion may cause hæmorrhage to take place from any or all parts of the body; a wasting consumption being thus produced that usually ends fatally.

The baths at Eupatoria have effected some wonderful cures, and their reputation is of course increasing.

The patient lies for some hours every day in the soft, healing muddy water, which, by degrees, makes a sort of artificial coating by leaving the sediment upon the body. The skin is thus protected until it can regain its proper health and thickness. We afterwards met a Russian in Sevastopol who had been quite cured by this singular remedy.

Immediately in front of the landing-place is the caravanserai, a long, low building, with galleries. It contains a number of small, empty rooms, of which any traveller may take possession for a night. We watched the arrival of a large party, who came in wearily with their tired horses and camels, having come across the Great Steppe, or wilderness, that for a hundred miles or more lies to the north of Eupatoria.

Side by side with the mosque, the walls almost joining, is the principal Greek church, and round it are the best houses, which we, on landing, thought very wretched; but having been brought to a proper degree of depression by a walk through the town, we found them quite comfortable as we returned.

It would be difficult to find a place more squalid and filthy than this miserable little town. Eyes and nose are equally offended; and after the delicate cleanliness so apparent in the Turks and their houses, Eupatoria and its inhabitants appeared the more revolting.

Men, women, and houses looked as if water had been a luxury unknown to them from the earliest days. Oil, oil everywhere—on the walls, in the clothes, in the air, even on the ground. One would have expected to see it running in the gutters, could anything run here, but everything liquid seems to stagnate, and turn into sticky mud. Nothing was clean except the kittens, and they may fairly claim to be counted amongst the population of the town, so numerous were they.

The bazaars were better supplied than might have been supposed from the poverty-stricken appearance of the place.

The bread was fairly good, and fruit very abundant. The melons, especially, were excellent, and exceedingly cheap. We bought some of the finest in the market for little more than two copecks (about a penny) apiece.

The day following our arrival we went on shore about six o'clock, in order to have a long drive into the Steppe. Whilst waiting for our conveyance we went into the Greek church, and found it crowded with people, it being the Feast of the Assumption.

The full dress of the Greek priests is very magnificent. One of those now officiating had a robe of silver tissue, with a large cape of crimson velvet, half covered with gold embroidery. The custom, also, of wearing the hair long adds much to the picturesque appearance of the Greek "papas."

The youngest of the three priests had a singularly beautiful face, in shape and colouring like one of Leonardo da Vinci's pictures of Our Saviour. The hair, wavy and silky as that of a woman, and of a reddish, or rather golden-brown shade, hung in rich masses over his shoulders, nearly down to his waist.

The congregation was composed principally of men of the lower classes, dressed in the ordinary costume of Russian peasants. This consists of a sheepskin coat, a cap of the same material, very full cloth trousers, and great leather boots.

Although well clad, and with no appearance of poverty about them, yet there was in the attitude and bearing of these men an expression of deep humility, almost amounting to slavishness, that was painful to see. Very remarkable, also, was the utter joylessness of the faces around. There was no lack of intelligence, but these poor people looked as if the very power of being happy or cheerful had died away within their hearts.

Occasionally during the service they prostrated themselves in the Turkish fashion, by touching the ground with their foreheads; but for the greater part of the time they were crossing themselves diligently.

No man could have crossed himself less than two or three hundred times during the hour we remained in the church.

Before the service had quite concluded, a sound, as if a lot of old saucepans had been dragged to the door, accompanied by the stamping of horses and the shouts of men, announced that our carriage had arrived, and on going out we found a wonderful-looking conveyance awaiting us. A long box, something like an unpainted hearse, had been fastened by bits of rope and bands of iron to a set of wheels which looked as if they had originally belonged to a gun-carriage; and it was evident that springs were a luxury not to be expected. There were no seats, but some straw, covered by a couple of sheepskins, had been put in for us to sit upon.

We climbed up, and arranged ourselves as well as we could, but with some dismal forebodings on the subject of fleas, which, unhappily, were fully realised.

We tumbled and bumped over a sort of track, passing through a wretched street of decayed warehouses, and almost equally ruinous huts, and then by a row of windmills, so small that they looked like children's toys, till we came to the open country, or steppe.

It would be difficult to imagine anything more desolate than the arid plain that stretches beyond Eupatoria, on the north side, as far as eye can reach.

It is half marsh, half sand, and for many months during the winter lies partially under water.

Here and there may be seen a patch of reedy grass, like an oasis in the desert. On one of these two Bactrian camels were feeding, and their uncouth forms and awkward movements were very appropriate adjuncts to the gloomy dreariness of the scene.

Bactrian camels differ from those of Egypt and Syria in having two humps instead of one; and being in general better bred, and consequently swifter than the animals in the latter countries, are of course more valuable.

A drive of a few miles satisfied our curiosity respecting the steppe. We might have journeyed on for days and have still seen the flat, desolate plain stretching far, far away with the same gloomy monotony of dreariness. So, finding that the cramp was seizing us, and that our bones were decidedly aching from the bumps and blows we got in consequence of the primitive construction of our vehicle, we turned back towards the sea.

Along the shore were still lying the remains of some of the French vessels wrecked here during the storm of the 14th of November, 1854, and a mast or two, sticking up from a sand-bank at no great distance, showed where some other unfortunate ships had more recently found a grave.

We had heard that there was a Jewish synagogue here well worth seeing, and also interesting, as being the favourite burial-place of many Rabbis of the Russian Jews. So, leaving the carriage at the entrance of the town, we dived into a perfect labyrinth of little, dark streets, even more unsavoury than those whose acquaintance we had already made.

Our guide halted under an ancient archway, and ringing a bell, in a few minutes the trap of a little grating was slipped aside, and a tremulous old voice asked who were the visitors, and what they wanted. The answer being satisfactory, bolts were withdrawn and chains let down, a small door opened, and we found ourselves in a deliciously clean, shady court, made dark and cool by trellises covered with vines, from which great bunches of rich purple grapes were hanging in tempting profusion. In the corners stood pots of the sweet clove-pink, and the sun's rays, softened by the shadowing vine-leaves, fell upon the marble pavement, beneath whose slabs lay the body of many a Rabbi well known in Jewish history. Some of those, who were now resting in their last sleep in this quiet spot, had died the death of martyrs in Poland and elsewhere, and, in secrecy and with much difficulty, their poor remains had been brought here to lie in peace amidst their brethren.

The synagogue was a room about forty feet square. The walls were ornamented with Hebrew sentences from the Old Testament, and in numerous little niches around lay the Bibles and Talmuds of the congregation. Before a screen at the upper end was a small table, covered with a cloth that was a mass of gold, embroidery, and seed pearls. On either side were desks, on which lay the Books of the Law, and above the screen stood the golden candlesticks with their seven mystical branches. Ostrich eggs and crimson horse-tails were suspended from the roof, as in a Turkish mosque, and the floor was covered with an unusual number of magnificent Persian rugs, laid one over the other.

As we passed through some other small courts and gardens, we saw several women peeping at us from behind the doors. At length two or three gained courage enough to show themselves, and very pretty they looked in their picturesque costume. They had white chemises, with large loose sleeves, bound with red round the throat and arms, and a broad border of the same colour on their short black petticoats. They wore on their heads a little fez with a bright purple tassel, and each fair Jewess had four or five thick plaits of hair hanging down almost to her feet. We were lost in admiration at the length and beauty of these tresses, but, alas! discovered that they were heirlooms, not growing on the heads, but sewn on to the fezzes of the wearers, and with care they may sometimes serve two, or even three generations.

Jews, as a class, are sometimes said to be oppressed and ill-treated in Russia, but certainly in Eupatoria they were the only people we saw who were clean and thoroughly well dressed, and whose houses appeared comfortable and comparatively free from oil.

The wind favoured us, and we had an excellent run from Eupatoria to Old Fort, where the English troops landed on the 14th of September, 1854. As we were rowing on shore the breeze shifted, and we suddenly found ourselves enveloped in a dense shower of locusts. The flight was so enormous that it quite darkened the air, and explained the meaning of a singular cloud we had been watching for some hours, thinking, as it came up, that it must bode either thunder or heavy rain.

It was sufficiently disagreeable to have these revolting animals falling upon one every second, but this annoyance was as nothing compared with the horror of the smell that assailed us when we came to the shore. Myriads of dead and dying locusts were lying in masses upon the ground. The day was intensely hot, and the sun, streaming upon the mass of decaying insects, seemed to draw a cloud of pestilential vapour from the ground, while every now and then a puff of sickening miasma came from a little piece of water close by, rightly called the Foetid Lake, from some peculiarity of the mud on its banks.

My curiosity was not strong enough to enable me to endure the horrors of a walk over the dead and dying animals, so I fled to the boat, and, under the protection of a thick cloak and huge umbrella, waited there until the others had seen enough.

For hours the yacht was passing through the swarm, or detachments of it. Such numbers of the disgusting insects fell on the deck that two men were constantly employed in sweeping them into the sea. Every window, every crevice, was kept carefully closed, for fear that one of them should get below. There is something inexpressibly revolting about these horrid animals. They fly, they crawl, and they cling, and, after having come in contact with them, we could well understand what a frightful infliction the plague of them in Egypt must have been. Wherever they pass they leave barrenness and pestilence. We hoped the flight we had met might be driven out to sea. It was a very large one, for long after we had passed through it, we could see the dark cloud extending along the horizon like hills.

Beyond Old Fort the country began to improve. The sandy plain gradually changed into gentle undulations, then rose to picturesque hills, and at last, in the distance, a range of fine mountains came in sight. Here and there a few small farmsteads, surrounded by patches of cultivated ground, showed that the soil was more genial than that around Eupatoria and Old Fort.

In the glow of a lovely sunset, the sea gently breaking in little waves upon the beach, the lark singing above the corn-fields, in all the quiet and repose of a summer evening, we came upon the scene of the most awful strife and carnage the world has seen in modern times.

As we lay in towards the shore, on our right was the steep bank up which the brave Zouaves forced their way; the pretty grass-field beyond, where a flock of sheep were so peacefully feeding, was the deadly slope where so many of the noble and gallant 23rd Welsh Fusiliers died a soldier's death. That fearful day is now a story of long ago—but what English heart can look upon the field of Alma and remain unmoved?

The chalk cliffs near the sea are about thirty feet high, and are curiously intersected by strata of red gravel. As the sun slowly sank, these cliffs caught his last rays, and were dyed so deep a crimson that we could almost fancy the battle had but been to-day, and that the long dark stains were indeed the blood so nobly shed by our gallant soldiers.

We hove-to opposite the mouth of the little river, and sent a boat on shore to see if we could land, but a Cossack, who had been suspiciously watching the movements of the yacht all day (and a long hot ride he must have had), rode rapidly down to the beach, and, pointing his lance in very warlike fashion at the men, clearly demonstrated that no landing must be attempted. The boatswain, who spoke Russ, tried to remonstrate, but an order had lately been sent from Odessa, that no person should be allowed to land on the coast without a permit, so, with our destination before us, we had to set sail and depart.

CHAPTER VIII.
SEVASTOPOL.

The next morning, soon after six a.m., we were awakened by the roar of cannon, and running on deck to ascertain the cause, found that the yacht was dashing along under a fresh breeze, and rapidly approaching the entrance to Sevastopol.

Wreaths of smoke were curling round Fort Constantine. We could hear the hissing of the shot as it fell into the sea, and such warlike sights and sounds almost made one fancy we had come in time for the siege; but drawing near, the ruins that lay around, the masts, and the bits of wreck sticking up in all parts of the harbour (making the navigation both difficult and dangerous), showed we had but arrived to see the *effects* of war.

Even after the lapse of so many years, the scene of desolation was extraordinary. The forts are not even in ruins. So completely have they been destroyed, that only masses of broken stones show the sites where they once stood. On the heights are rows of handsome houses, or palace-like barracks, still roofless, the walls shattered, and grass growing thickly between the stones.

The Russians seem to have had as yet no heart or inclination to attempt seriously the work of restoration. A few houses have been made habitable, some rebuilt, but whole quarters have been left as they were at the termination of the siege. In some streets, where apparently a perfect storm of shot and shell must have descended, the walls of the houses left are so shattered that it seems almost unsafe to walk about amongst them—they look as if a gust of wind must bring them down.

The principal church of St. Nicholas has been restored, and houses have been built for the governor, admiral, and principal officials; but of the beautiful public buildings and magnificent palaces of which Sevastopol was once so proud nothing now is left but the scorched, battered, and defaced skeletons. Some of these poor remains still retain traces of their former grandeur. Here and there a bit of tarnished gilding, pieces of what was once rich sculpture, traces of painting, the remains of stone or marble staircases, still cling to the crumbling walls. Never again, in all probability, will this once beautiful city regain the prosperity and position she enjoyed before the fatal war that brought about her destruction.

Sevastopol was the pet child of several successive Emperors, and unheard-of were the sums expended, not only on the naval and military defences of a place for many years deemed impregnable, but also for the decoration and improvements of her streets and public buildings.

To insure the houses being well and handsomely built, and to assist also many of the naval and military officials, whose pay is generally so small that they can barely subsist upon it, the Russian government had for many years adopted the following system:—

The land, both in the town and immediately around it, was Crown property. Supposing an officer wished to build a house, he sent a plan of it to the Minister of the Interior, and an estimate made by the government architect. Should the plan be approved, and if the house would cost, say, 20,000 roubles, the government would advance at once 10,000 roubles, and in two years time 10,000 more. This money was lent without interest for five years, but had then to be repaid by instalments.

Should the whole sum of 20,000 roubles not have been repaid within ten years, the house then became the property of the Crown. This regulation, however, was seldom carried into effect, and the borrower was generally permitted to pay interest for the money until he could pay off the principal. As the houses were large and let in apartments, as in Paris, the rents obtained were in most cases far greater than necessary to repay the interest of the money expended.

In the old, merry days Sevastopol was a very gay place. Being the principal port of the Black Sea, the Plymouth in fact of the Empire of the Czar, it was the great rendezvous of the fleet, and a large number of naval officers and their families were always resident. The immense garrison also made an important addition to the society, and many of the South Russian families passed their winter in Sevastopol, the climate being much more temperate than at either Odessa or Simpheropol.

Sevastopol, therefore, was considered, after St. Petersburg and Moscow, the gayest and most brilliant town in Russia. Its nearness also to the imperial villa at Yalta made the official appointments eagerly sought after.

But these gay balls, dinners, concerts, &c., are now only things of the past. The inhabitants can be counted by tens instead of by thousands, and but for the families of those whose duty obliges them to remain, the town would speedily cease to be. Dull as Sevastopol generally is, it was duller than usual during our stay, for several of the principal officials had been summoned to Odessa to attend two of the imperial princes. Those who remained, however, seemed as if they could not be kind enough, or friendly enough, to travellers from a country who a few years back had been so terrible an enemy.

There has ever been such kind feeling and such friendship between Russia and England that it must always be painful to an Englishman to think circumstances should have forced us into a cruel war with an old and steady friend.

The day after our arrival we got three droskies to take us to the Redan and the neighbouring heights. Crimean droskies are like very low gigs, and hold two persons besides the driver, who sits upon a small box or perch high above the body of the carriage. One of the horses is in shafts, with a wooden arch hung with bells over his head, the other is in traces on the left side. When well driven this horse canters while the other trots, and however rough and uneven the road, the pace is generally tremendous.

The drivers were strange wild creatures, with long unkempt beards, and hair that flew out behind them like a cloud as we raced along. They wore coarse frieze coats, with long full skirts coming down to their heels, and loose trousers tucked into great Wellington boots, so redolent of musk and train oil that every time their owner kicked the plank beneath his feet, in his energy to overcome some unusual difficulty, an odour was wafted to us that was far from resembling those that come from Araby the Blest.

Our progress was both noisy and exciting. On coming to a bad place the drivers stood up, stamped with excitement, shouting to their team, and addressing them in a stream of terms both of endearment and abuse. The horses tossed their heads as they struggled and plunged, the bells jangling furiously, and we could only hold tight as the light carriage bounded over hole or mound.

Carriage-hire is dear, each drosky costing about one rouble and a half an hour; a rouble is nearly 3s. 4d. in English money.

The dust during the summer in and about Sevastopol is quite remarkable, and can be only equalled by the mud in winter. The soil is principally of a description of chalk that rapidly pulverises during dry weather, and equally rapidly dissolves during wet. The result is that in summer the town and country seem wrapped in clouds of fine penetrating dust, and during winter the mud is ancle-deep.

Within ten minutes of our start we were as white as millers, and half-choked besides, as, perfectly regardless of our wishes and requests, the drivers occasionally amused themselves by racing, or else insisted upon keeping close to the wheels of the preceding carriage.

After passing through street after street of ruins, we found ourselves in a narrow ravine immediately beneath the Redan, and at about a quarter of a mile from the town came to the first or most advanced English trench. Of course years have gradually levelled the soil, and now it is like a small dry ditch, but even had the mound raised been three times the height it now is, it seemed amazing that so slight an amount of earth could have been sufficient to protect the soldiers from the rain of shot so unceasingly poured from the town. Even with gabions on the top, the men could not have stood upright in the trench.

About fifty yards up the valley was a mound of earth with two "dents" in it. This had been an English battery of two guns, and the dents marked the places where the cannon had stood. Higher up was another trench, then another battery, and so on, until, the defile making a turn, the town was no longer commanded.

Now and then we passed a small enclosure surrounded by rough walls, or came to a heap of earth with a few stones piled upon its summit. These are the resting-places of many of our soldiers. There are no names, in a few more years even these slight traces will be obliterated, and the earth, once so deeply dyed with their blood, will give no token of the brave hearts she has taken to her bosom. These humble graves, the only record of so many unknown but gallant men, all of whom had died fighting for their country, appeal even more powerfully to the feelings than the long line of grand monuments on Cathcart's Hill, though many great and distinguished names are recorded there.

Many can understand and share Lord Nelson's feelings when he exclaimed, "A peerage, or Westminster Abbey;" but how hard to die for one's country, knowing that that country will not even remember the name of its poor servant!

After winding up the valley for another mile and a half, we left the road, and ascending a little down or grass field found ourselves within half a mile of the Redan. Strange to say, though we had mounted to a considerable height, but very little of the town was visible from the spot where we were.

Seen from the sea, Sevastopol appears to stand in an amphitheatre of hills, that apparently command it on every side; but, in fact, there are only two heights that really do so—namely, those of the Malakoff and the Redan. The view was extensive, and we could see, for a considerable distance inland, over an undulating but now barren country. The ground around had been so torn and rent by the iron storm of shot and shell, that it looked as if it had been badly ploughed by awkward giants, but time has now covered the ugly wounds with a soft vesture of grass and thyme. Nature has done all the reparation that has been made. We could see no traces of cultivation in any direction, neither were any cattle or sheep to be seen feeding on the miles of short, sweet down grass that would have been so suitable for them; but where war lays her destroying hand, the labours and improvements of centuries are destroyed in as many hours.

A sandy track led to the Redan, the ground at every step giving more and more evidence of the deadly struggle that had taken place. In every direction huge ragged holes and fissures showed where mines had been sprung, and monstrous rents in the ground, close to the fort, marked where some battery had poured a stream of fiery shot, that had torn its way through earth, and stone, and iron with appalling strength.

Bullets and pieces of shot and shell are still to be found in abundance, and women and children are constantly employed in turning over the earth in search of these relics, and also of the small brass crosses, one of which is always worn by every Russian soldier.

Standing on the edge of the ditch, the desperate nature of the attack could be better appreciated. The ditch was about fifteen feet deep, with a tremendous *chevaux-de-frise* at the bottom, and the guns of the fort were so numerous that the embrasures were not more than a few feet apart. It is difficult to imagine a more appalling position than to have to lead troops on to such certain death. Our guide, who had belonged to the Land Transport Corps, saw the attack made.

The most advanced English trench was about a hundred and fifty feet from the Redan, and it was from here the final rush was made. On came the officers closely followed by the devoted regiments, and through the deadly hail of shot and grape that was pouring from the Russian guns, the attacking columns rushed up the fatal slope. But few of these gallant men entered the breach, the terrific fire mowed them down by hundreds, and in a few seconds the ground was covered with the dead and dying. "Never," said our informant, "could he forget the hideous yells, shouts, and shrieks that filled the air."

The first man who raised the English standard on the Russian bastion was Captain Robert Preston, but he had scarcely waved it in the air when he fell, pierced by twenty wounds. Our guide saw him fall, on a heap of dead Russians, with the gabions on fire by his side.

Inside the fort the number of mines that had been sprung had so riddled the ground that much caution was required to avoid falling into the great holes.

The sun had now set, twilight in these countries is very short, for darkness soon comes on, and just when the grey duskiness of evening gave additional gloom to the dreary scene of desolation and ruin around, quietly stealing from behind the broken wall of the nearest graveyard came creeping a lean, savage jackal. So noiseless and so stealthy were his movements, that at times his dark grey form could scarcely be distinguished from the dark grey stones by which he stole so cautiously. Breathlessly we watched the savage creature as he prowled along. The wind blowing strongly towards us, for a few minutes we were undetected, but very soon a slight rustle made by one of the party betrayed our neighbourhood, and in a second, with a vicious snarl and snap, the animal was bounding off, with long loping strides, towards the open country. In wild countries troops of jackals always form part of the camp-followers of a great army. As the vulture and the crow scent carrion, so does the instinct of the jackal tell him where human bodies are interred, and unless the surrounding walls are high and strong, many a burial-place has been desecrated by these savage and cowardly animals.

CHAPTER IX.
TRACES OF WAR.

We started one fine, sunny morning, at eight o'clock, for a long expedition to Cathcart's Hill and St. George's Monastery. We left the town by the valley beneath the Redan, but instead of taking the turn to the left that leads to the fort, followed the course of the defile until we arrived at some table land, where are the remains of the English Picket House. Close by is the burial-ground of the Light Division. It is surrounded by low but well-built walls. Neglect, however, and the rapid growth of weeds have made many of the inscriptions, and even some of the graves, invisible. In the centre stands a pyramid, bearing inscriptions both in English and Russ to the officers and men belonging to the Light Division. One monument had the following words, deeply cut in the stone: "Sacred to the memory of the officers, non-commissioned officers, and men of the 77th Regiment, who lost their lives in the service of their country during the campaign in the Crimea. This monument is erected by the officers of the Regiment, as a humble tribute of respect to the fortitude and bravery of their fallen comrades."

Pushing aside the grass and rank weeds, we found the names of many friends, and with the aid of parasols and sticks, cleared some graves from the tangled growth of years, and planted upon them tufts of sweet-scented thyme and a little blue flower very like the forget-me-not. From some we gathered a few coarse wild-flowers, and even blades of grass, to bear home to mothers whose hearts are still aching for the brave young dead who have but a soldier's grave so far from home and from those who loved them. Many we had known well, in the brightest hours of their youth and happiness, were sleeping here in bloody graves. No words can adequately express the depression of spirits which must come after passing hours in going from burial-ground to burial-ground, only to see where those, once so loved in life, so honoured in their death, now lie—uncared for, unthought of—in cemeteries that, instead of being evidences of a nation's gratitude and reverence, are now untended and forgotten, a tangled mass of weeds, and but fit homes for the jackal and the fox.

Leaving the Woronzoff road on the right, we came to a knoll, or patch of rising ground, from whence an excellent view of the town can be had. It was here that the non-fighting visitors usually took up their position, for not only could a good general view of the camps and town be obtained, but, with glasses, it was easy to see the people walking in the streets.

The road passes by a small village, where, standing in the midst of some neat enclosures, with a well-filled farmyard at its rear, is a low one-storied house.

This unpretending little building was once the head-quarters of the English staff, and here poor Lord Raglan breathed his last.

Notwithstanding the severe losses and sufferings that were caused to its owners by their home and property being seized by the enemy, Monsieur and Madame B—— receive with kindness and hospitality any English who may wander here. We are, however, at present the only foreigners who have visited Sevastopol this year.

In a small sitting-room a marble slab has been let into the wall, over the place where the bed stood on which Lord Raglan died. In the wood of the folding doors are cut the names of Field-Marshal Lord Raglan, General Simpson, and Sir William Codrington. The temporary grave in which the body of the noble old soldier was placed previous to its removal to England, has also been well cared for. Willows hang over the spot, and it is surrounded by a border of rose-bushes and flowers.

A tale of the troubles caused by war is always sad to hear, and the family, at whose hospitable board we were seated, had been absolutely ruined by their losses, and were now attempting to begin the world afresh; but though Monsieur B—— is an energetic farmer and works, his wife says, early and late, he has hitherto reaped but little reward for his toil. Life, commerce, energy, have alike deserted Sevastopol, and there is but little or no market either there or in the neighbourhood.

Poor little Madame B——, with tears in her pretty eyes, deplored in fervent language the loss of her comfortable home. Her husband was with his regiment on the north side, when the rapid approach of the allies obliged her and her children to fly for safety to Simpheropol. She left a house, well, almost luxuriously furnished, and returned at the end of the war to find but bare walls—not even a chair had been left. The farm and garden gone—gone also the woods and valuable vineyards, the very roots of which had been torn up and burnt. Our graceful little hostess, however, with a tender regard for the feelings of her stranger guests, hastened to add that the ruin of the place was not owing to the English army, whose generals had kindly striven to save and to spare as much as possible, but to those human locusts, the Tartar camp-followers.

From Cathcart's Hill we drove to Kerani, a desolate little village lying amongst the hills near Balaclava. There were about half-a-dozen half-ruined wooden hovels, and a couple of better-class houses, although these were also built of wood. To one of these we were most kindly welcomed by Colonel S——.

The long sloping roofs, weighted by large stones, and the peculiarly small windows, only seen in stormy countries, showed how severe the winters must sometimes be here, and we were told that, though cold is seldom of long continuance, and though snow rarely remains for many days upon the ground, yet the gales of wind during the winter months are of extraordinary violence, the long narrow gullies with which the hills are intersected acting as funnels, down which the raging tempest hurries with increasing fury and strength. In general, however, the gales, though severe, are short, and in the memory of man no such terrible winters had been known as those experienced by our troops during the two years they were in the Crimea. Never before had such intense cold been known; never before had the storms been so prolonged and incessant. Direct manifestations, it was believed by the lower order of Russians, that Providence itself was against the unrighteous invasion of the land.

We had a pleasant luncheon at Colonel S———'s, and the live stock of the yacht was increased by the kind gift (rather to Mr. Harvey's horror) of a pair of quite lovely geese. We had not believed the usually despised goose could be so beautiful a bird. These geese were as white as snow, had backs and wings covered with long curling feathers like ostrich plumes, and had bright pink bills and feet; but for their unfortunate voices they might have set up for swans. Our dear birds, however, did not approve of being summarily torn from the paternal pond and packed in a basket, so they hissed and cackled all the rest of the day in a thoroughly goose-like and provoking manner.

From Kerani we went to St. George's Monastery—a long low building, standing apparently in a flat, ugly country; but on passing through an archway, and descending a few steps, an enchanting view was before us.

The convent is built upon the extreme edge of a steep wooded cliff overhanging a little bay. Paths had been cut through the wood, and wound down between trees and rocks to the verge of the sea, where tiny waves were coming quietly in upon a shining beach, trickling back amongst the many-coloured shells and stones with a pleasant murmur, most refreshing on such a burningly hot day. But the sun was now glowing with almost blinding heat upon this the western side, so we retired into the interior of the building until the intolerable glare should have somewhat subsided.

There are now only five brethren of the order living at St. George. Since the war the number has greatly diminished, and some are required for another house at Simpheropol. We were invited to have some tea, an offer we thankfully accepted, and while it was getting ready were asked to pay a visit to the cells. They were fairly comfortable, indeed better than may be found in many religious houses in Italy and France, that have not so strict a rule as the Greek convents.

Each brother was provided with a table, a stool, some boards on tressels for a bed, a mattress (certainly very thin), and a blanket; but what can monks wish for more? In the Greek Church, the severity of monastic life consists principally in the length and rigid observance of the frequent fasts, and in the small amount of sleep that is permitted. There is scarcely a religious house in which meat is ever eaten, and twice a week, during the long fast of Easter, only one meal a day is allowed, consisting of beans boiled with oil.

As there are no inns in this part of the world, excepting in towns, monasteries answer the purpose, and though payment is not permitted, each traveller, ere he departs, is expected to drop an offering into the poor-box.

While waiting for the tea, some water was brought from the famous spring of St. George. It is celebrated for miles around, and well deserves its fame. Fresh, sparkling, and cold as if iced, it was really nectar. Well for us it was so, for we needed some little compensation for the disappointment that awaited us with respect to the much-wished-for, long-promised tea. The eagerly-expected beverage, when it did at last arrive, was brought in tumblers, without either milk or sugar, and being a very strong decoction of something bitter, between sloes and haystalks, it was so like a horrid medicine called "black draught," that nothing but the strongest exertion of good manners could enable one to swallow even a few drops.

At six o'clock we went into chapel for the Ave Maria. The chapel is a neat little building, detached from the monastery, and has some altar-pieces remarkably well painted. The pictures of the saints were covered with plaques of gold and silver in *alto-relievo*, and had glories of precious stones around their heads.

The congregation was very limited, for it consisted of only three brethren, the sacristan, and one old woman, but the service was got over with wonderful speed, though with no apparent disrespect of manner. Vespers over, we were shown the chapel. Behind the altar-screen was an exceedingly good picture of The Crucifixion, but as it was in a part of the building that women are not allowed to profane by their unholy presence, my sister and I had to remain on the other side of the altar, the monks most good-naturedly drawing aside curtains, and trying to give us as good a view as possible.

The evening had by this time become cool and pleasant, so we strolled down the cliffs to look at the ancient chapel, the hanging gardens, and the renowned spring. Excepting its antiquity, the former possesses no interest; it is a very small stone building, supposed to have been erected by the Genoese when they occupied this country, but both in form and decoration it is remarkably simple.

The stream poured forth from the rock with delicious freshness, dashing, in a series of tiny cascades, from terrace to terrace, ever sprinkling with a shower of brilliant drops the mosses and tender ferns that grew on its banks, until, on reaching the good monks' gardens, it flowed decorously through appointed channels. Then, its duties over, it gave one glad bound, as a miniature waterfall, over the rocks into the sea, and was lost in the embrace of its mighty mother. The terrace-gardens are beautifully kept, for the monks labour in them unceasingly. The good fathers are the principal doctors of the district, and grow, therefore, not only vegetables for their own use, but most of the plants and herbs required for medicinal purposes.

It was late before we returned to Sevastopol, but the drive back in the cool night air was very refreshing. As we descended the heights into the town, we could see the bright lights of our many-coloured little Turkish lanterns shining a cheerful welcome to us from the yacht. It is worth while to feel very tired, in order to experience the inexpressible feeling of comfort that comes over one when, on getting on board, we find the tea-table invitingly prepared on deck, the samovar bubbling merrily under the teapot, the little kitten ready for a game of play, and everything speaking of the snugness and rest of home.

The country immediately around Sevastopol looks rather pretty, and is pleasant enough in fine weather. The air on the heights is fresh and invigorating, and the clearness of the atmosphere gives a charm to the distant views both over sea and land. A very few hours' rain, however, makes the place quite detestable, for it is impossible to move out, either in the town or beyond it, without having to wade through a perfect slough of sticky white mud. The misery and illness that must have prevailed in the camps, after days of continued down-pour, can be easily imagined.

Our first visit to Marshal Pelissier's head-quarters was made on one of these melancholy days. A Scotch mist, that had been driven in from the sea, gradually changed into a steady, soaking rain, but we were too far from home to turn back, and being fortunately well cloaked and shod, in forlorn procession we waded through puddles and mud from graveyard to graveyard. To the credit of the French nation, they are far better tended than ours. Still the scene was gloomy enough to suit the gloomy day. The huts, formerly inhabited by the troops, have fallen into ruins, and the wood is rotting on the ground. Here and there are huge mounds of broken bottles and other refuse, and near them again are great pits, where infected clothing, &c., were burnt during the time the cholera was raging. The French head-quarters seem to have been very well placed, for though on a commanding height, they must have been in a great measure protected from the cruel north wind that blew with such bitter severity into the English tents on Cathcart's Hill.

Even black clouds and depressing rain could not make us insensible to the beauty of the valley of Tchernaia. It lies deep amongst rocks, with a fine range of chalk hills in the distance. The long white lines on their rugged sides looked like snow whenever a straggling ray of light fell upon them through the dark and heavy mass of clouds. Quite at the upper end of the valley, where it turns to the right towards Balaclava, are two low hills, covered with the ruins of Sir Colin Campbell's camp. The long flat piece of ground beneath these will be ever memorable as the scene of the famous charge of cavalry. The little plain forms a sort of amphitheatre, as it is partly surrounded at one end by a series of hillocks or rising ground. On these commanding positions were posted the Russian guns. Even an inexperienced eye could see at a glance that the devoted regiments must have been rushing to certain death. It seems marvellous that men can be so trained to passive obedience, that, without a murmur, they hurry to their doom. Every officer, at any rate, was probably aware that the heroic effort could but be a useless sacrifice of human life. What must have been the agony of those who were forced to look on at such frightful and unnecessary carnage, powerless to prevent, and powerless to aid?

Balaclava is a quaint little place, completely shut in by hills and rocks. The entrance to the harbour from the sea is very difficult to find even when quite close to it, so curiously does the channel twist and turn about. It must have been once a better-class village than any we had yet seen, for the church, though in a dilapidated state, is large, and the houses, though partly in ruins, are of good size. Some have been repaired, and most are inhabited, but everything speaks of ruin and discouragement. The landing-place is rotting in the water, the warehouses made by the English are rotting on the shore, and the dirty, dreary-looking people seem as if they were decaying away in their poverty and hopelessness.

Drinking is unhappily the prevailing vice in the Crimea. We rarely went on shore without seeing several tipsy men. Towards evening one generally meets wives and daughters dutifully wheeling their husbands and fathers home in barrows. Yesterday we met a procession of five being thus brought back in triumph from some prolonged carouse. To the credit of the fair sex, it is but just to say we have not seen one woman so degradingly overcome.

The Russian women we have hitherto seen, though they cannot be called pretty, have generally very pleasant faces. Their voices are sweet and low, and the gentleness of their manner is very prepossessing. It is impossible, however, not to feel that so much timidity probably originates in the harsh treatment they experience in their homes, for the men, though humble and cringing when addressing their superiors, are coarse and boorish to their inferiors. These observations, of course, only refer to the lower classes. Amongst the higher ranks, Russians of both sexes are quite remarkable for their charm of manner and peculiar talents for society. The extraordinary kindness we received from every family whose acquaintance we made during our stay in the Crimea, quite endeared these kind people to us, and personal experience enables us to say that Russian friendship does not limit itself to charming manners alone.

During our stay in Sevastopol, we became well acquainted with several of the ladies who had remained in the town during the siege. With the exception of one, all were wives or daughters of officers in command, and who, with noble devotion, had refused to leave their relations in the hour of danger. With unwearied zeal they laboured in the hospitals, for, notwithstanding every effort, the amount of attendance was lamentably deficient, and it was only possible to provide for the more pressing need of the sufferers. All unite in saying that the courage and fortitude of these ladies were beyond praise. Many of them were quite young girls, but, regardless of personal danger, they not only visited the hospitals, but wherever illness or suffering required their presence these true Sisters of Mercy were to be found. Death was ever before them, for who could tell where or when would come the fatal shot? Day and night shells were exploding in the devoted town. No spot was safe. When sleeping in their homes, or praying in their churches, the fiery shot might come crashing through the walls, dealing death and destruction around. The narrow escapes related to us might fill a volume. One lady had barely left the side of a wounded man, when a shot came through the roof, instantly terminating the sufferings of the patient, and injuring another in a neighbouring bed. One charming young girl, Mademoiselle Androvna R——, daughter of a general commanding a division, had been in Sevastopol from the beginning of the siege until the end. She was an only daughter, but her father and two brothers were soldiers, and she remained with them to be, as they said, "their guardian angel." Although so many years have now elapsed, Androvna was strongly moved as she spoke of the anguish of that terrible time. Parting almost daily, in ignorance as to whether they should ever meet again, when again they met the little family felt as if it were impossible they could all be much longer spared. Sometimes a brother would have to proceed to an advanced post, and then it might be days before they would know whether he was amongst the living or the dead.

One day, as Androvna was on her way to the hospital, she met the sad procession of the wounded as they were carried in, and found her youngest brother amongst the number; but the young man, though he bears the marks of a fearful sword-cut across the face, and has lost an arm, still lives, to love and cherish his devoted sister, who nursed him through his sufferings with the tenderest care. Who could think of personal danger when in such agony of anxiety for loved ones, who were hourly exposed to far greater peril? So great was the strain upon the nerves, that Androvna says she believed she should have gone mad but for the supporting duty she felt it to attend the sick and wounded in the hospitals. By the bedside of these poor sufferers self was for a time forgotten, and when she could occasionally creep away to some neighbouring church, and on her knees before her patron saint lay down her burden of sorrow and anxiety, then peace and courage returned to her heavily-laden heart.

She had, however, personally some narrow escapes. One day, for instance, she was sitting in her room, with a pet dog lying at her feet, when a shot came crashing through part of the house. The little animal at her side was crushed to death by a falling piece of wood, but the young girl happily escaped with a few slight bruises.

CHAPTER X.
VALLEY OF TCHERNAIA.

Not being at all satisfied with only having seen the fair valley of Tchernaia in the gloom of rain and wind, we resolved to try whether the glow of a fine summer day would not heighten its charms. One warm sunny morning, therefore, we put a basket of provisions and a Russian dictionary in the yacht's cutter, and set off to breakfast under the trees in a pleasant grass field beyond Inkerman. The wind was contrary, so we had to row across the harbour, and for about a mile up the river Tcherné; it then became favourable, and strong enough to enable us to stem the little current, so, setting a sail, we glided up the stream most pleasantly and rapidly.

Grèbe, divers, and other water-fowl were continually darting in and out of the masses of reeds that grew along the banks, and at a sudden turn of the river a great eagle, probably disturbed at his morning meal, rose slowly in the air, and sailed away majestically towards the mountains.

It was very early; the morning breeze was deliciously cool and fresh, and as we lazily reclined on our comfortable seats, listening to the soft sound of the water as it rippled against the bows of the boat, or to the merry voices of the children as they chattered to their favourite Domenico, it seemed as if life could offer nothing pleasanter than to be thus gliding away in the summer sunshine towards unknown scenes and beauties. Whatever might have been the worthy Domenico's faults with respect to his masters, he was admired and adored by every child who came near him.

He had an art, quite peculiar to himself, for turning everything he saw into something not intended by nature. Leaves, flowers, sticks, stalks, became astonishing musical instruments after passing through his cunning hands, and he would weave rushes, leaves, and flowers into garlands, baskets, and a variety of pretty things, with a rapidity and skill that was quite marvellous, and of course to the intense delight of the little folk around him. His pipes and whistles, also, blew better and with greater shrillness than any pipes and whistles that ever were known. Should occasion require he could be an admirable cook; he could sing buffo songs with a talent worthy of San Carlino itself; he could make clothes; he could improvise clever verses; but unfortunately his inspirations would come to him at unlucky moments, and while he was meditating a stanza more sublime than usual a pile of plates or dishes would fall from his hands, and his soaring spirit would be brought back to earth by an energetic remonstrance on his carelessness.

Happily he had not been in a poetic vein when he packed the breakfast basket. The only thing omitted was some fruit, a want that was soon supplied, for we passed a small house where the trellises were absolutely laden with grapes, and we bought a large basket of them for something under half a rouble.

We continued our course up the river, passing between water-meadows that had quite a park-like appearance from some fine old trees that had happily escaped destruction. The many ranges of hills also that could be seen as the valley opened were very beautiful, for though hardly lofty enough to deserve the name of mountains, the line of the more distant was rugged and bold, and in the clear atmosphere tier upon tier could be seen, till the last faded away in the blue distance.

While we went to look at the ruined village of Inkerman the sail was taken in, and as, owing to the large beds of rushes, the stream was rapidly narrowing, we took to the oars again, until we arrived opposite a small church and a few little houses that had been hewn out of the cliff itself.

The Tcherné divides here into several channels, all too shallow for the boat, so we landed, and establishing ourselves under some large trees, found a pleasant shelter from the sun, whose rays had now become both fierce and overpowering. We spread our breakfast on the grass, close to a delicious little ford, where the water, quite put out of temper by the impeding stones, dashed and tossed itself about in sparkles of brilliant rage. At length, throwing itself down in a fierce little set of passionate cascades, it recovered its calmness, and quietly subsided into the gentle stream beneath. Can anything be more beautiful than such a stream? and what delight greater than to rest thus under the shadow of great trees, watching the sunshine as it plays on bank, and tree, and meadow, and to know also one is far away from the working, weary troubles and pleasures of the world?

Seated on the warm, dry turf, we passed a couple of hours very luxuriously, and somewhat idly. In fact, some of the party indulged in a little slumber, a weakness quite to be forgiven, for the day and place seemed alike made for repose. Not a breath stirred the air, the leaves hung motionless on the trees, the bees hummed drowsily among the flowers. The very birds were silent, the reed-sparrow alone sending forth her monotonous piping note from some neighbouring bushes, and the tinkling sound of the falling water made the most soothing music imaginable. However, after a time we crossed the stream by means of the little ford, and ascended the cliff to the church and village; but church and houses were alike deserted. The door of the former was locked and the houses were empty. Not a soul was to be seen anywhere. We hunted about some time in hopes of finding the key—for we had been told the chapel was well worth seeing, and contained some curious old pictures—but in vain. The door was so old and shaky that a vigorous blow would have broken it open, but not thinking so felonious a mode of entrance suitable to the character of the edifice, we walked back towards Inkerman by a path that gave us beautiful views of the valley and mountains.

The village of Inkerman no longer exists; a few blackened walls alone mark its site.

The battle was fought on the rising ground immediately above the valley, and the earth still retains many memorials of the bloody strife. Half buried in the soil, close to a low wall, we found part of a broken sword; and any number of flattened bullets, buttons, and portions of soldiers' decorations could be easily had by digging up the earth with parasol handles or sticks. On the highest point has been placed a simple stone monument to the memory of all the combatants who fell in that terrible struggle. English, French, and Russians there share alike in the honour of that fatal day; and truly a soldier's glory seems but a very little thing.

A short walk along the rising ground brought us to all that is now left of the Malakoff. There are two ditches round it, but neither of them is as deep as that which surrounds the Redan. The fort itself, however, is very much larger, and in the centre are the ruins of a low, flat tower. It was originally bomb-proof, but the French blew it up when they obtained possession, and now barely half of the building remains standing.

The Malakoff so completely overlooks and commands the town that even the non-combatant can perceive how useless must have been any attempt to hold Sevastopol when once this, the key as it were to the position, was in possession of the allies. Those who held the Malakoff and the Redan had virtually Sevastopol, for shot and shell from these forts could be poured like hail into the devoted town. These two great outposts lost by the Russians, all further struggle on their part must have been hopeless.

Count K—— tells us that in fact Prince Menschikoff had resolved to evacuate the town, and retire to the north side, when the Quarries and the Mamelon had fallen into the hands of the allies; and he would have done so before the attack on the Malakoff was made, but for positive orders from St. Petersburg to hold the town as long as possible.

As far as we could judge, the general opinion amongst the Russian officers was that the chief error Russia committed was in allowing the allies to land undisturbed. Probably subsequent events confirmed their views, but all seemed to think, had the French and English met with a vigorous resistance when they disembarked, Sevastopol would never have been invested. Unhappily for them, the higher authorities at St. Petersburg were so firmly convinced that Sevastopol and her forts were impregnable, that it was hoped, could the allies be led on to make an attack upon the outworks, that not only would they be repulsed, but that the annihilation of the whole invading army would be the necessary consequence. Those generals who knew the place, and who had some doubts as to the "impossibility" of taking it from the land side, were not listened to. Any attack from the sea must have been in vain.

Notwithstanding the kindness of our friends—notwithstanding the fineness of the weather (for we had but few rainy days during the many weeks we passed at Sevastopol), we longed to leave the place. Words cannot adequately express the profound gloom and depression that weigh down the spirits after any lengthened residence in the town of death. At first, the great interest of seeing a place become so famous in history, the excitement of visiting spot after spot renowned for deeds of chivalrous daring unequalled in modern times, support the mind; but, after a time, the one story told by every house, by every field, by every grave—of untimely death, of man's love of destruction, and of man's lust for blood—oppresses the heart with a weight of sadness that becomes almost unendurable.

Our favourite walk on many a bright summer's evening was to stroll up to the Redan, and there we would seat ourselves on a little grassy mound, the last resting-place probably of a dead man, and gaze on the destroyed city below.

The larks would be singing gaily over our heads, the crickets chirping around; but if we pushed away the grass, or disturbed the earth ever so little, how many records would meet the eye of the deadly strife that had raged on the very spot where we were now so quietly seated, while the extraordinary, almost awful silence of the great city made one indeed feel that it was now but a city of tombs.

A little below us, on the right, stand the once lordly Alexandra barracks—a building at one time unequalled of its kind in grandeur and extent. Now the bare walls alone remain; the sky can be seen through the long lines of windows. In lieu of roof, a few blackened rafters project here and there, like monstrous gibbets, and the masses of *débris* around show how thoroughly the work of destruction has been carried out.

It is beyond measure depressing to walk through miles of ruined streets; and, if so painful to the stranger, how heartbreaking must it be to Russians, to see beautiful buildings, once the pride of the country, hopelessly defaced and destroyed.

The water-gate by which we land when coming from the yacht must once have been a great ornament to the beautiful town, for it is still lovely even in its ruin. It resembles the colonnade of an ancient Greek temple, and is approached by a broad flight of shallow steps. These, however, as well as the fine mosaic pavement, have been broken and defaced, the roof has been battered in by shells, the statues have been overthrown and broken, and scarcely a column remains uninjured.

Near this gate is the opera-house, or rather what is left of it. It was formerly a large building with a long Greek façade; but the walls are now shattered, and blackened by fire, and the columns and decorations lie broken on the ground.

The hospital is almost the only place that has not suffered severely from the effects of the fiery hail that was so incessantly pouring into the town. A flag showed where the unhappy wounded were lying, and as far as possible the building was spared by the besiegers; still its scorched and blackened sides and some yawning holes tell that it did not altogether escape.

Near it is a small chapel, now almost a ruin, a sad memento of the sufferings of some of our poor fellows. Towards the latter end of the siege, space, air, attendants, and surgical aid were all lamentably inefficient to supply even the pressing needs of the masses of wounded who were brought in.

During the last few days also the confusion that reigned in the town almost overcame discipline. No sooner was the evacuation decided upon than orders were given that, not only were the Russian wounded to be conveyed immediately to the north side, but that all valuables that could not be removed at the same time were to be burnt during the last night, not only to prevent them from falling into the hands of the enemy, but that the smoke should conceal the movements of the Russians; for this reason also many portions of the town were set on fire. It may easily be imagined, therefore, that there was but little time or attention given to the unhappy wounded of the enemy who were to be left behind; so, when the allies entered the deserted city, terrible were some of the scenes that met their eyes. In this very chapel a harrowing sight was beheld, for many of our poor countrymen were lying here unheeded and untended, yet alive, with the dead in heaps around them.

The harbour of Sevastopol is supposed to be unequalled for size, depth of water, and security. It very much resembles Plymouth in the number of arms that branch off from the main channel. The entrance is so broad and easy of access that vessels can run in for shelter with almost any wind, and when inside the forts the various channels are so completely landlocked that ships can lie in perfect safety whatever sea may rage outside.

The navigation within is, however, now somewhat difficult, as the Russians sank nearly all the vessels then in port when the English fleet appeared before Sevastopol, and though most of the wrecks have been raised, still enough remain to require skilful pilotage to avoid the hidden dangers.

The only cheerful place in all Sevastopol (out-of-door cheerfulness, that is— not the many friendly houses that were always open to us) was a small promenade, consisting of the ghost of once beautiful pleasure-gardens, where the band played on fine evenings.

Here the few people left in Sevastopol would assemble at sunset to listen to the excellent music and enjoy the cool evening air. As night came on the scene would be very pretty. Darkness hid the ruins around, so that the stars seemed only to shine on glistening white monuments; the lights from the vessels in the harbour quivered like lines of silver as they were reflected in the gently rippling water; and when at last the whole glory of heaven was unfolded, the dark-blue arch above seemed one dazzling array of brilliant stars.

Those who have not seen them can form no idea of the glorious beauty of the nights in these southern countries. The stars do not twinkle, they blaze with bright silver light, and the eye in vain endeavours to penetrate the glittering maze of which the heavens seem formed.

We find that this summer is considered at Sevastopol rather hotter than the average, but we have seldom found the heat very oppressive. The sun is powerful during the day, and often beats fiercely upon the dry, parched soil. It is well therefore, if possible, to avoid exposing oneself to the great heat of midday; but at sunset the fresh sea-breeze always sets in, and the nights are cool and invigorating.

Amongst the many advantages yachtsmen enjoy over travellers by land is the inestimable one of being nearly always sure of a breeze at night, and none but those who have travelled much in warm climates can tell how great that blessing is. Fatigue and heat during the day can well be borne when one is sure of a quiet and refreshing sleep. Another comfort also is comparative freedom from mosquitoes and flies. How often when we have been doomed to spend the night in some wretched inn or house, half-stifled by the heat and bad smells, tormented beyond endurance by swarms of mosquitoes, sand-flies, fleas, or perhaps worse, have we sighed for the little cabins with their comfortable elastic mattresses, the fresh clean sheets, and the cool night wind that would have been fanning us as we rocked in our dear *Claymore*!

Having once found ourselves in Malta during the hot months of July and August, and having felt great compassion for the unfortunate English soldiers as they marched up and down, under a blazing sun, in all the misery and magnificence of the tight regulation scarlet coat, with their throats braced up by a stiff collar, we much admired the simple and comfortable uniform worn during summer by the Russian troops. The men have a complete suit of grey cotton, with peaked caps of the same material. The officers wear white jean, with a band of scarlet round their caps, and sometimes a sash of the same colour.

CHAPTER XI.
A RUSSIAN INTERIOR.

Leaving Sevastopol one afternoon, a favourable breeze carried us rapidly back to the Alma, and being now provided with the necessary permit, we could land without danger of being impaled by our enemy, the Cossack. We had also brought a letter of introduction to Count B——, a neighbouring proprietor, and, having sent it to the village, we landed, and strolled along the beach, looking at the heights the Zouaves had climbed.

Count B—— speedily arrived, kindly answering the letter in person, and bringing his carriage with him; so in a few minutes we found ourselves seated behind two spirited little Tartar horses, and away we went across the plain, perfectly regardless of the absence of road. We passed several large stack-yards, full of substantial ricks of hay and corn, where wild-looking Tartars were thrashing out the grain—a simple process, accomplished by fastening heavy blocks of wood to Tartar ponies, who were driven at full gallop round and round the enclosure.

The women wore their long hair in innumerable plaits, hanging below their fez caps, and showed their Mohammedan tendencies by partly veiling their faces as we passed. Feminine curiosity made them peep at us from sheltered corners, though they seldom ventured to show themselves completely.

We turned into one of these farmyards, and found ourselves in front of a little one-storied house, standing near a mass of blackened ruins. Here we were most kindly received by Madame B—— and a large family party, consisting of an aunt, Mademoiselle M——, a sister-in-law, two young ladies, several children, and three gentlemen. Most of the party talked French, and we were welcomed with charming kindness.

Soon after our arrival tea was proposed, which, thanks to the universal samovar, is almost always good in Russia. This time the pleasant meal seemed doubly excellent, for, besides grapes and water melons, there was a great bowl of cream, a luxury we had not seen for a long time. Milk, as well as butter, is almost unattainable in Sevastopol. The evening, though pleasant, was very warm, so we were delighted to see that, instead of being prepared in the little house, the hospitable tea-table was spread in the farmyard, and there we sat, surrounded by cows, chickens, turkeys, and dogs, in quite a patriarchal fashion, and enjoying ourselves greatly, for the charming family with whom we were had the rare art of viewing everything *en rose*, and while bearing their reverses with dignified simplicity, yet took whatever little pleasure came in their way with hearty and unaffected delight.

Milking was going on, and noticing the beauty of the cows, of which there were about twenty, we asked our hostess how much milk they gave a day. She did not know, nor did any one, she said, keep an account, for there is a superstition in the Crimea that should the milk be measured the cows immediately become dry.

We were kindly pressed to remain the night, but we wished to return to the children, who had been left on board the yacht. Besides, the house seemed so *very* small, compared with the party already assembled, that we could scarcely believe in the "possibility" of our being taken in, whatever good-will there might be. We looked around, thinking there must be some other house besides the very little one before us, but no, nothing was to be seen but some Tartar huts, a few cow-hovels, and the blackened ruins. So, with many thanks, we adhered to our original intention, and then the greater part of the party proposed to accompany us to the sea-shore.

A large, powerful horse—a fine creature, but of a fiery and impetuous nature—was with some difficulty harnessed to a lofty gig, or "heavenly chariot," into which I was invited to mount. I did so, though, it must be confessed, with some inward trepidation. In another moment our hostess was by my side, and the fiery steed stood on his hind legs, as if he meant to "pose" for ever as a statue for a "horse rampant."

The young ladies, without any preparation, jumped on two Tartar ponies; the rest of the party got into the other carriage. Our energetic animal condescended to come down on his forelegs, and, with a bound that almost took away my breath, off we set—"over brook, over byre"—going across country in the dark in the most astonishing fashion. To the very last moment that fiery steed acted well up to his character; snorting, plunging, and exerting himself most unnecessarily when any obstruction came in his way. However, the fair charioteer, twisting the reins twice round her hands, seemed fully equal to her task, and so away we went, with glorious indifference to holes, mounds, or other little impediments.

The young ladies rode admirably. It could have been no easy matter, and needed no little courage, to sit so steadily, galloping at such a headlong pace, on a dark night, over rough ground full of holes. However, we all arrived quite safely at the sea-shore, and found our kind friends had brought us a supply of vegetables, fruit, butter, and cream that made us rich for many days.

When we rejoined our hospitable entertainers the following morning the mystery of the sleeping accommodation was explained. The little house only possessed two rooms divided by a passage. All the men slept in one room, the ladies had the other; the governess being the best off, as she had a shelf to herself in the passage. These kind people had really intended to share their house with us, and proposed to give us one room and the passage, taking the little governess into their already crowded room, and sending the luckless men to find shelter where they could.

The "Heavenly Chariot" was again made ready, the mighty steed being more frisky than ever, as he felt the cheerful influence of the fresh morning air, and after breakfast we all, some in carriages, some on horseback, went to visit the field of the battle of the Alma.

Standing immediately beneath the Heights they appear exceedingly steep, and difficult to climb, especially one would think when exposed to a galling fire, but this very steepness proved the salvation of the Zouaves.

Once arrived at the foot of the cliffs, they were *within* the range of the Russian guns, and these active fellows, who climb like cats, were speedily at the top, and engaged in a hand-to-hand combat with their foe.

Our host, who had been on Prince Menschikoff's staff, said that the Russians committed two fatal mistakes early in the day.

In his opinion the Russian guns should have opened fire when the allies were crossing the river, and when their line consequently was somewhat broken and disorganised. Unhappily, there was difference of opinion and dissension amongst the Russian generals, and therefore, marvellous to relate, no very precise orders were issued on the important morning, so the favourable moment was lost.

Deeming, also, their position impregnable, the Russians were probably paralysed by the suddenness and vigour of the attack.

Another almost equally fatal error was committed later in the day. Several Russian regiments, instead of waiting to receive the enemy on the commanding position they occupied on the Heights, rashly descended to a sort of second terrace, a few feet below the summit of the cliff; a most disastrous move on their part, for when the Zouaves and light infantry swarmed up the rocks the miserable Russians were bayoneted and cut down without a chance of retreat.

In fact most accounts tend to show that want of organization, and the want of supreme military power on the spot, contributed quite as much as the vigour of the attack to the loss of the battle of the Alma, and the subsequent fall of Sevastopol.

The Russians do full justice to the dauntless courage and brilliant military talents of their foes, but the destruction of Sevastopol lies heavy on their hearts, for the higher classes think her fall was as much brought about by faults at home as by the intrepid valour of the besiegers.

In the early part of the war, intrigues, it is said, were rife at the Russian Court, and the plans of the Crimean generals were constantly interfered with and made of no effect by contradictory orders from St. Petersburg. It was believed by the Emperor that the garrison in Sevastopol was so immense that in itself it formed a large and efficient army. It was believed that stores and all other requisites were there in such abundance that the town was capable of sustaining unassisted a protracted siege of even years, whereas so great had been the venality practised that many regiments, supposed to be fully manned, barely existed but in name.

So far from being able to support a long siege, the vast store-houses were more than half empty, and with respect even to ammunition and arms the supply was lamentably inadequate. It is said also that some of the cannon and shells were made of *wood*.

When all the present generation has passed away, and when the history of the Crimean war will only be classed among the histories of the past, many who read the story will feel a deep compassion for the mighty Emperor whose heart broke when he at length knew the fatal truth. His cherished town—his impregnable fortress—the pride of Russia—the key-stone, as it were, to all his ambitious projects, must fall into the hands of the enemy for want of troops, food, ammunition—for want of the very things with which he supposed it had been so well supplied. Supplies were sent, troops were sent, but in what condition could they arrive after having traversed a country the width of Europe, in the depth of winter, without railways, and nearly without towns?

The Russians are essentially a brave and noble people; it is impossible to live amongst them and not admire and like them. They love their sovereign with a personal devotion almost beyond bounds, and they can and have fought for their country to the death, but they know their system of government is very faulty.

Late events especially have led them to see how the present system tends to much oppression and venality, and that though the Emperor really labours earnestly and unweariedly for the welfare of his subjects, yet it is impossible any one man can sufficiently superintend and legislate for so vast an empire.

On the gentle slope of a pretty grass hill, where a flock of sheep were peacefully grazing, is the simple stone erected to the memory of the noble 23rd Welsh Fusileers, and a few feet from it are a number of long, narrow trenches, the edges roughly marked by stones, the graves of their gallant enemies.

Many hundred Russians lie here, but neither cross nor monument records *their* names. In a few more years the stones will be all dispersed, and nothing will then mark the spot where so frightful an amount of human life was sacrificed.

We again descended the valley to visit the tomb of Captain Horace Cust. It is owing to the kind care of our hostess that it is still in existence. When the family returned to Burlinck after the war, Madame B—— found the stone thrown down, defaced, and half buried in the earth, but she had it repaired and by a curious accident Captain Cust's brother arrived in Sevastopol and came to see the little monument only the day after it had been replaced. But for Madame B——'s kindness few of the graves would have been respected, for the Tartars are very destructive, and carry off everything that they think has any value.

Count B—— has been a great sufferer from the war. His property near the Alma was worth about twenty thousand roubles a year. Now it barely yields enough to supply the family with more than simple necessaries. Formerly they spent the winter in the old Russian capital, Moscow, now they go for a few months to Simpheropol, and live here as simple farmers during the rest of the year, and a farm-life in the Crimea does not imply the comforts that are to be found on most English homesteads.

Though our host has lost so much—for besides his house several farms were burnt, the cattle seized, and the vineyards and woods destroyed—there are very many others who have been still more unfortunate. For instance, his aunt, Mlle. M——, before the war began was the owner of a fine property with a large house in the valley of Tchernaia, but long ere the siege was over she found herself absolutely ruined.

It seems wonderful that the landing of large bodies of foreign troops should have caused so little alarm amongst the inhabitants of the Crimea, but far from fearing danger for themselves, the prevailing feeling was apparently astonishment that any army should be so rash as thus to court its own destruction. Sevastopol was believed to be so safe that it is said some adventurous female spirits wished to proceed there, to witness in person the discomfiture and defeat of the allied forces.

When the allies landed, Mlle. M——, being in bad health, was unwilling to leave home. Sevastopol was so near that there seemed but little or no danger that a retreat into the town could be cut off. The Heights of the Alma also were supposed to present a formidable if not an insurmountable obstacle to the advance of the enemy, so Mlle. M—— and her household remained at Tchernaia.

"One evening," said Mlle. M——, "we were sitting round the card-table playing loto, but I was a little uneasy that a messenger I had sent to one of my nephews in Sevastopol had not yet returned. A sudden noise was heard in the hall; and my niece was hurrying to the door of the saloon, when it was hastily thrown open by the messenger, accompanied by several of the servants, who with scared faces and in breathless accents announced that a party of foreign cavalry had been seen to enter a wood only a few versts from the house, and that if we meant to escape there was not a moment to lose.

"In the hurry and alarm of such a departure it was not possible to take away with us more than mere necessaries, and though most of the valuables, such as silver and pictures, had happily been sent to Simpheropol many weeks previously, still," said poor Mlle. M——, with a deep sigh, "I left my dear home full of every comfort and luxury. I dare not lament," said the kind old lady, as a few tears ran slowly down her cheeks, "over my poor furniture and little treasures when I remember the dreadful sorrows that came to us afterwards, but it gives a bitter pang to an old woman like myself, on returning to a once dear and happy home, to find only a heap of blackened ruins,"

She did not mention what we knew, namely, that all the remains of her little fortune had gone to help the sick and wounded, for when she retreated into Sevastopol she joined the devoted band of the Sisters of Mercy, and eventually became one of the lady-superintendents of hospitals. In spite of feeble health, in spite of the constant danger to which she was exposed, this good woman remained steadily at her post until the troops withdrew to the north side.

We did not like to ask many questions, for, like all who shared in those terrible duties, the scenes they then saw seem to have been too dreadful to bear being dwelt on, and the kind creature could not relate without tears some of the sad incidents that had come under her notice. Some of her patients were poor little fellows, whose manhood all deserted them under the pain of their wounds, and these she held in her motherly arms till their cries ceased, and death mercifully took them from their sufferings.

Like Androvna R——, Mlle. M—— said that all sense of personal danger became so soon merged in higher anxieties, that even the narrow escapes of many of the nurses ceased to excite much interest. The trial was to hear cries for the help that could not be given—to see terrible sufferings without the possibility of affording relief. In spite of heroic courage, nature would occasionally give way at the sight of wounds and mutilations of unusual horror, but still the devoted band of women never slackened their efforts, and laboured unweariedly at their divine and holy task.

The Russian soldier seems to be as patient in the hospital as he is obedient and brave on the battle-field. The poor fellows, unless very young, bore their sufferings with great fortitude, and Mlle. M—— said it was most touching to see their unselfishness and consideration for others. From her account there was an excellent staff of surgeons, though scarcely numerous enough for the requirements of such vast numbers of wounded. There appears also to have been a good supply of medicine, but there was a considerable deficiency of linen and bandages. The main cause of the great suffering arose from the very limited amount of accommodation.

The hospitals were frightfully crowded, and consequently the air became so impure that the wounds could not heal, and gangrene and disease carried off as many Russians as the guns of the enemy.

Mlle. M―― was the unconscious heroine of a little story that went the round of most English and French journals. It was reported that Prince Menschikoff's carriage had fallen into the hands of the allies, and many were the jokes that were made respecting a certain pretty pink satin bonnet, and other articles appertaining to a lady's toilet, that had been found packed therein. Unfortunately for the lovers of romance, both carriage and bonnet belonged to our friend Mlle. M――, who, though both charming and good-looking for her age, is no longer a young woman, being between sixty and seventy. The carriage in question had been packed to go to Simpheropol, but when the hurried flight became necessary it was found too heavy for such a rapid journey, and it had to be abandoned to its fate.

Mlle. M―― wishes to sell her estate at Tchernaia, but landed property in the neighbourhood of Sevastopol has so deteriorated in value that she has not yet succeeded in finding a purchaser, and it may be some years before she will be able to do so. It is almost equally impossible to let it. One farm is now in cultivation, and a few grass fields are let for grazing sheep, but the greater portion of the land has been left untilled and useless.

It was at first expected that the Government would have paid five per cent. on all property destroyed, but the expenses of the war have been so infinitely greater than was originally supposed, that the unfortunate proprietors say now they shall think themselves well off if they succeed in obtaining one per cent. of indemnification. It will be many years before the country will be able to recover the effects of so violent a blow.

We left the Alma, with a storm muttering in the distance, and every probability of wind, but soon after passing Sevastopol the breeze dropped and it fell dead calm. Not a puff filled the sails, which flapped idly against the masts; but somehow or other we drifted on, and the coast scenery was so fine that we did not regret the slow progress.

Magnificent cliffs, valleys wooded nearly to the water's edge, and pretty villages made quite a panorama of beautiful views, whose general aspect reminded us much of the Undercliff of the Isle of Wight, only on a far grander scale.

Aloupka, Prince Woronzoff's place, is most lovely. The house is built of grey granite, and seemed to us exceedingly picturesque, though architects and connoisseurs would probably shake their heads dismally over it, as a specimen of bad taste.

The architecture, it must be admitted, is certainly *"very mixed,"* being partly Gothic, partly Moorish, and altogether modern; but the numerous pinnacles and towers, and the long façade of buildings rising above the magnificent woods, have a remarkably good effect. A series of broad terraces descend from the house half way down to the sea; beautiful gardens, full of rare shrubs and flowers, lie on each side of the house, and the woods and park stretch away for miles along the cliffs.

General Malthoff has a very fine place, more in-land; and a few miles beyond Yalta is Orianda, the Empress's villa.

Yalta itself is a tiny village, lying close to the sea, and surrounded by, almost buried in, a magnificent amphitheatre of mountains. The village contains about fifty houses, all nestling round a little wooded hill, on the top of which stands the church, its bright green cupolas and gilded pinnacles looking resplendent in the brilliant sunshine.

The villas, however, are the glory of Yalta. On every slope, peeping through openings in the dark green woods, are the pretty white houses. Almost all are half covered with creepers, and standing in gardens now gay with flowers, have an air of comfort and *Heimlichkeit*, or *homeishness* (if such a word can be permitted), to which we have long been strangers.

The lovely woods—the green grass—the fresh mountain air make Yalta quite a little paradise. We had the additional pleasure, also, of finding friends here—Prince and Princess B——, who came on board immediately, and whose affectionate welcome, and cheery talk of old times and old friends, made this distant place feel quite like home.

We had also another visitor, an American, who, seeing the English flag, came on board to borrow some money. He was one of the unfavourable specimens of Yankeyism who do so much discredit to their country, and whose principle is to ask for a gate when they want a bit of wood. The modest request was for £25, which Mr. Harvey declined to lend, but I suppose his heart being touched by seeing a foreigner so far from home, and in distress, he gave him enough to take him to Sevastopol, with a note to an American there, who would help him if necessary. Our friend then said, however, that he heard we were going on to Circassia, and as it was very difficult to get there, he thought he might as well take "a spell" with us, as he could fix himself down in the yacht very well. As he spoke, the sensible little craft made a sudden roll and a lurch, that caused such an internal convulsion in our would-be companion that he threw himself into the boat and departed, happily for us to return no more.

The next day we went with the B———s and a large party to Orianda. Our conveyance was an immense char-à-banc, that could hold quite a dozen people. There were scarcely any springs to speak of, but luckily the roads were excellent.

The drive from Yalta to Orianda is one of the most beautiful I have ever seen. Sometimes the road wound up and down hills, and then we could look over the steep banks of woods or vines upon the intensely blue sea below. Sometimes it passed between great overhanging rocks that almost met overhead; then, again, it would cross sunny bits of rough common, or wind down narrow deep lanes where the damp coolness was delicious, and where the high banks seemed hung with ferns, and woodbines, and other plants that love the warm moist shade.

We passed a charming house of Count Potocki's. The broad verandah was quite festooned with passion flowers, roses, and the bright lilac blossom of the Clematis Jackmanni. The gardens and grounds were as well kept as any English home could be. The neat hedges, gravel walks, and smooth lawns made us think we must be in England again.

We left the carriage at the lodge gates and walked down the beautiful road to Orianda, sometimes passing under trellises of vines, where the purple grapes were hanging in delicious profusion, then going through woods and avenues of fine trees.

The rays of the setting sun were now streaming through every opening, making the old Scotch firs look all aflame in the glorious light.

The villa is a large, white Grecian building, not handsome enough for a palace nor pretty enough for a country house. There are some fine rooms, rather grand and very gloomy. The pleasantest sitting-room was a hall, painted and decorated like a Pompeian court, with a fountain in the centre, surrounded by flowers and ferns.

The gardens and terraces make the delight of the place. Vines, myrtles, and magnolia-trees are trained over arches, and under their fragrant shade, the air cooled by innumerable fountains, how pleasantly must the summer days pass! What an enchanting change from hot, dusty St. Petersburg!

The present Empress has not yet paid this pretty place a visit, but the Grand-Duchess Constantine came for several months one summer. Her Imperial Highness seems to have made herself universally popular; her parties enlivened the whole neighbourhood, and she is spoken of by all classes with the heartiest affection.

Within an hour after sunset the wind became bitterly cold, and every cloak and shawl was called into requisition during the drive home. This sudden change of temperature is the only drawback to Yalta, and invalids who come here for health must carefully avoid exposing themselves to the night-air. The dew also falls very heavily; therefore here, as in Italy, the hour after sunset is a dangerous period. Later in the night, for those who are strong, the fresh wind is very invigorating.

Yalta is so favourite a spot that people come even from Petersburg to spend the summer here. It gives one some idea of the enormous extent of Russia to know that it is a fortnight's journey, travelling night and day, to get from Yalta to St. Petersburg.

Thanks to our kind friends, the B——s, we have seen all the prettiest villas in the neighbourhood. Count Narisckine has a very lovely estate. There are also some beautiful places now unhappily shut up and uninhabited, the owners having been ruined by the war. Land and houses can now be bought very cheap, but unfortunately Yalta is too far from England to make it available as a summer residence.

Prince Woronzoff has a very fine property at Aloupka, and a nearer approach made it even more beautiful than we had thought it from the yacht. The house stands in a magnificent position on a narrow ridge of table-land between the cliffs and the sea. Great dark woods stretch around it for miles, and the rock scenery is quite superb. Our Russian friends did not, however, share our enthusiasm, and thought the more cultivated, smiling scenery round Yalta infinitely more beautiful.

On arriving at Aloupka we drove through a fine gateway into a courtyard, on one side of which was the house, on the other were the offices and stables. Immediately within the portico was seen the hospitable "Salve," set in large letters in the mosaic pavement. A glass door opened into the hall, a moderate-sized room, panelled with oak and hung round with family portraits. Amongst them was a picture of the late Lady Pembroke. Princess Woronzoff's boudoir and a few other small rooms were on one side of the entrance; on the other was the great dining-hall, a large and lofty room with three recesses: two of these were occupied by fireplaces, the other had a small fountain, an agreeable addition to a dining-room on a hot day.

Another glass door led to a very pretty room—half saloon, half conservatory. Climbing plants were trained up the columns and over the frames of the looking-glasses. Masses of flowers were arranged in groups upon the marble floor, while thick Persian carpets and every sort of comfortable lounge and easy chair made the apartment the very perfection of a summer sitting-room.

Russians have quite a talent for decorating their rooms with flowers and shrubs, and should nothing better be forthcoming, branches of trees make a background for the little cluster of plants that are placed in every corner. Dwarf palms or tree-ferns have a charming effect when crowning a group of flowering shrubs.

On the storey below were the salons and library. The latter was a large and comfortable room, well filled with books, the tables being covered with the newest French and English publications.

Prince and Princess Woronzoff were away, so we soon finished our inspection of the house. Though thoroughly comfortable, it is much smaller in reality than its appearance from the sea would lead one to expect. Seen from a distance the long, imposing façade makes it look quite like a palace.

The grounds, however, gained in beauty from a nearer view. Great flights of steps lead to broad terraces, on which are the most delicious gardens and lawns that imagination can picture. Every flower to be found in England and Italy grows here in perfection, revelling in an admirable climate and in an admirable soil.

In front of the house was a stone colonnade, up every pillar of which were trained climbing plants of unusual beauty. One in particular was especially lovely, a species of *Mandevillia superba*. There must have been many hundreds of the snowy white fragrant flowers, shining like stars from the mass of glossy dark foliage.

In the centre of the colonnade was a portico as high as the house itself, having a roof fretted and gilt after the fashion of the Moorish courts in the Alhambra. Light balconies, supported by clusters of columns, projected on either side, and comfortable sofas were arranged amongst the little wood of orange and citron trees below.

It was a day and a scene when life alone seemed a delicious blessing. The soft breeze barely whispered amongst the leaves, a few doves were tenderly cooing in the garden below, the very fountains seemed unwilling to disturb the magic quiet, and their waters fell soothingly into the marble basins, as if they were also hushing nature to rest. Every now and then the sweet south wind sighed gently over the wide expanse of sea, and then came upon the ear the trickle, trickle of the little waves, as they rippled back amongst the pebbles of the beach, and as the wind softly touched the trees overhead, down came a fragrant rain of the snowy leaves of the orange-flowers, making the ground white with the lovely blossoms.

Talking of old times and old scenes, hours passed like minutes in this enchanting and enchanted spot, and we had forgotten how long we had been enjoying a feeling of divine repose that one longed might last for ever, when the sun sank below the horizon. For a few minutes there was a great blaze and glory of light, and then a grey damp gloom stole over the landscape that warned us to be gone. Perhaps, even then, we should have lingered longer than was warranted by strict prudence, but we were all engaged to have supper with the T——s, and knew the sportsmen, who had gone out quail shooting, would have returned with clamorous appetites. The rattling wheels of our char-à-banc were no sooner heard in the village than out flew all the hungry party to know what had detained us; but the roasted quails were so good, and so were the little newly-baked sponge-cakes, that every one rejoiced in being hungry, and a merry evening finished our pleasant day.

CHAPTER XII.
CIRCASSIA.

Having seen all that was to be seen in the immediate neighbourhood of Yalta, it was unanimously agreed that the yacht should be put in requisition, and that an expedition should be made to Oursouf, a place on the coast, lately bought by Prince B———.

The day was fine, and the sea apparently smooth, but there was a little ground-swell that made us somewhat anxious about the happiness of our non-seafaring friends. Prince B——— was an old sailor, but his wife such a bad one that she never ventured on board a vessel under way. We were also very doubtful as to the sailing powers of Prince T——— and his sister. Count and Countess N——— had sailed with us before, and we knew they were proof, but we much feared the S———s and G———s were doomed to suffer. However, with admirable courage, all came on board at the time appointed, and we set sail.

While the wind lasted all went well, but unhappily about mid-day the breeze dropped, and then, one after another, the poor ladies fell victims to the levelling malady of sea-sickness, and the cabins presented sad spectacles of suffering pleasure-seekers.

Most fortunately Prince T——— was not ill. Had he been so, we dared not picture to ourselves what would have been his mental as well as his physical sufferings, for he had come on board in a new and superb Tartar costume! We were speechless with amazement as the resplendent vision appeared on deck. Even our captain and Charlie could scarcely maintain a dignified silence, but Prince B——— could not contain his feelings. "Pourquoi le diable, T———, êtes-vous venu en costume de bal?" burst involuntarily from his lips. Happily our guest was ridicule-proof, for his toilette was the pride and happiness of his life, and he frequently astonished the quiet inhabitants of Yalta by appearing in four fresh suits a day. Only yesterday he had paid us a visit in a complete costume of plaid. Coat, waistcoat, trousers, linen, cap, even the pocket handkerchief, displayed the same somewhat remarkable checked pattern. The unwonted and gorgeous toilette that appeared to-day was, however, very little adapted for a nautical expedition. Crimson satin trousers, a similar jacket, magnificently embroidered in gold, and large loose sleeves made of fine cambric, however beautiful in themselves, certainly seemed out of place on the Black Sea, especially as the day was neither hot nor sunny. Our poor friend's bare arms soon looked pinched and blue with cold, but we dared not suggest either cloak or shawl for fear of injuring the well-starched beauty of the transparent sleeves.

However, at last the sun came out from behind the clouds, the air became warm, so did the poor arms, the breeze revived, the suffering ladies got better and appeared on deck, and in due time we arrived at Oursouf. It was a beautiful spot, quite close to the sea, and as wild as it was beautiful.

On the slope of a neighbouring hill is Massandra, another property belonging to the Woronzoff family. On another hill, called Anaka, is a model nursery-garden, established by Count Woronzoff when he was Governor of South Russia, and still kept up by Government. Every description of tree, shrub, and flower that can be grown in the climate is to be found in this nursery. Any one wishing to make vineyards, plantations, or gardens can buy the plants, with the advantage of learning the sort of tree, shrub, &c., which may be best adapted to the soil for which they are required.

All this part of what may be called the Undercliff of the Crimea seems peculiarly adapted for the culture of the vine. Sheltered by a range of mountains, as well as by almost perpendicular cliffs, from the keen north wind, the long slopes of rich soil seem to invite the formation of vineyards. The grapes that are now produced are excellent, and many sorts of wine have already been made.

Several of the Rhine wines have been so closely imitated—some even say excelled—that sanguine persons predict that in time the Crimean wines will rank higher than the Rhenish. Be that as it may, it seems a pity that the Russian growers should be content in many instances to give German names to their produce, instead of creating their own class of wines.

A sort of liqueur, something like Constantia, is highly prized by connoisseurs, but at present this is only produced in the private vineyards of the Bariatinsky and Woronzoff families, and at Orianda, and cannot be purchased.

Prince Woronzoff, who appears to have been a wise and enlightened governor, had a favourite scheme for bringing large districts into cultivation as vineyards. Unhappily, the war took place ere he could put his project in execution, and the country is now so impoverished and thrown back that it will be years before it can recover from the shock.

Oursouf is a little Tartar town, built on the slope of a steep hill, and close to an enormous rock, on the top of which are some ruins, said to have been once a castle.

A few miles inland rises the grand mountain of the Acondagh, so called from its outline being supposed to resemble a crouching bear. "Acon" means bear; "dagh" signifies mountain. Clouds were flitting over the summits of the range, so the likeness, if it existed, was invisible to our eyes.

Prince B—— has bought a small property a few versts from the village, and having lived much abroad, he intends building a perfect Italian villa, so as to introduce a mode of architecture which he believes will be remarkably well adapted both to the country and climate. At present the foundations only have been dug, but should our good fortune bring us here again in a few years, we hope to find our kind friend established in his retired home.

To those who do not object to pitch their tents away from the haunts of companionable man, this little estate offers every charm that can well be desired. The scenery is as beautiful as it is magnificent.

A lovely little wooded glen runs up from the sea, far away into the mountains, that gradually become steeper and steeper, until the stately Tchatar-Dagh appears in the distance, its rugged sides partly covered with forest, and its lofty peaks crowned with eternal snow.

A rapid stream winds its way through the valley, sometimes dashing down in rapid cascades, then lingering in dark and shady pools, whose banks seem the chosen home of every sort of beautiful fern. The *Osmunda regalis* grows to a size almost unknown in England, and tufts of many kinds of the delicate maiden-hair nestle between the stones wherever the spray of the waterfalls can reach their feathery branches. In the spring the lilies of the valley must carpet the ground. In some sheltered spots we found several varieties of large white lilies, and the autumnal cyclamen revels in the rich sandy soil.

Wild vines had climbed up many of the trees. The purple bunches looked very beautiful amongst the foliage, but the wild vine is dangerous in its close affection, and almost always destroys the poor tree that it honours with its notice.

On returning to the beach, we found the boat surrounded by a crowd of Tartars, who were looking at the sailors with mingled admiration and awe.

The wind was fair for the little home-voyage, but though the sea was not really rough, still there was sufficient movement to make some of our poor friends very miserable, and it was a relief to all parties when they were once more safely landed at Yalta. Those who were not ill remained on board for supper, whist, and music; and to our surprise, amongst these good sailors was the wearer of the Tartar costume.

It blew fresh all night, and a bank of heavy, dark clouds to windward warned us that better shelter must be sought than can be found at Yalta. Unfortunately there is no roadstead here, and the anchorage is by no means secure.

Our captain has been very restless and uneasy for the last two days, and can find no charms in a place where half-a-dozen anchors, as he says, would not hold the yacht should it come on to blow. So to-night we are to say good-bye to all our kind friends, to the green fields and to the pretty villas at Yalta.

Pleasant, cheerful little place, in all probability we shall never see you again, but amongst all the sunny memories our rovings have given us, few will be more sunny, more smiling than the remembrance of our days with you.

We spent the last day on shore with our friends happily, though somewhat sadly, and when we parted in the evening bore away with us not only the remembrance of many affectionate words, but a little souvenir from each of the kind hearts who had given such a sincere welcome to their English friends.

We left Yalta on the night of the 13th of September, with a fresh, favourable breeze. About seven o'clock on the morning of the 16th, the worthy Domenico came knocking at all the cabin doors. "La terra, Eccellenza; si vede alfine la terra." The good news brought us speedily on deck.

A lovely day and a smooth sea welcomed us to Circassia. How often we had talked about this enchanting, but far distant country—how often we had longed to see it, never imagining that such a wild dream could ever be realised; and now, before us, bright in the light of a fresh, dewy morning, lay our land of promise—the true "land of the citron and myrtle."

There are some things so beautiful that one shrinks from describing them. Words cannot paint the loveliness that is seen by the eye. To say that we saw before us a country that possessed, with the tender charm of English woodland scenery, the rich glow of the Italian landscape, and the grand majesty of Alpine ranges, gives but a feeble idea of the delicious beauty of the land we were gazing on. The light, the colouring, the exquisite effect of the soft mists as they slowly arose from the valleys, can be better imagined than described, but as we looked, we thought, Here is a land where Nature has in truth perfected her handiwork!

The yacht was moving gently on, there was barely a ripple on the water, and, seemingly, we were within a stone's throw of the shore. A little sandy beach ran along the edge of the sea, then rose banks all mossy and ferny, with undulating grass-fields and conical hills, with great clumps of oak and beech trees scattered about. Then came a region of dark fir-woods, mingled with the tender green of the weeping birches. Farther away still were steep hills and rugged mountains, their sides all covered with vast forests, stretching away far as the eye could reach, whilst above their dark shaggy masses rose the majestic peaks of a distant range, glistening white in their dazzling covering of eternal snow. Cattle and sheep were wandering over the rich pastures, but peaceful as the country appeared, peace is, in reality, the blessing most unknown to it. War is constantly raging, and the smiling plain and pretty thickets before us have been the scene of many a fierce struggle.

We longed to land. The boat was being lowered for the purpose, when luckily for us, as we afterwards discovered, a breeze sprang up, and we continued our course towards Soukoum-Kalé. Had we gone on shore, in all probability we should have been taken prisoners by the hostile Circassians (who hold this part of the country), carried up into the mountains, and compelled to pay a considerable sum before our involuntary sojourn amongst them had ended.

A species of guerilla warfare is incessantly going on between the inhabitants in these remote parts and the Russians. The former consider all Europeans as enemies, and though the Russians are nominally masters of the country, the Circassians still possess amongst the mountains some strongholds that are almost impregnable.

Whenever they have a chance, they make captures, on account of the ransoms they usually obtain. Should the prisoner be of any importance, he generally prefers paying a moderate sum, rather than endure months of miserable imprisonment. As to the common soldiers, they are usually shot, their value being but small.

Had we been made prisoners, it would, of course, have been possible to appeal both to the English and Russian Governments; but the journeys to and from Constantinople and St. Petersburg are very long, and as it would require some weeks to procure the necessary money, we should have had to lead a wretched existence amongst the mountains, making more experiences about wild Circassian life than would probably have pleased us.

There is an English consul at Soukoum, established since the Crimean war, but it is almost an honorary appointment, as Soukoum has no trade; and though Mr. D—— has deservedly the greatest influence amongst the Russians, he is powerless as regards the insurgent Circassians, and even had the Russian general sent troops to our assistance, what can soldiers do against wandering bands, who have no homes, nothing to lose, and whose simple wants are supplied by the natural products of the country?

Near the sea-shore is a very curious old church, called Pitsunda, standing quite alone miles away from any fort, or even traces of village. Tradition says it was built during the reign of Constantine, but nothing certain is known as to its origin. It was, however, repaired towards the latter end of the thirteenth century, and just before the last war with Turkey commenced, the Russians had made preparations for restoring it completely. Fine stone and marble had been brought from a considerable distance for the purpose, and we could see some partially-worked blocks still lying around. A magnificent cross in white marble, that had retained many traces of the rich sculpture of the fifteenth century, fell a victim to the fanaticism of the Turks. They shattered it into a thousand pieces, besides defacing the interior of the building as much as possible.

Even the Circassians (who are supposed to have no religion) had always respected this church, and it is really grievous that so fine a relic of antiquity should be falling into ruins.

As the day drew to its close the little breeze dropped, and the sea rested so calmly in its deep tranquillity, that not a ripple disturbed its mirror-like surface. The very forests appeared to be slumbering in the sun. A pile of light fleecy clouds that had been slowly flitting about all day changed to a soft crimson, and floated on a sky that shaded from intense blue to the most brilliant rose-colour. Then a shower of gold seemed to fall, and the clouds changed into a long veil of pink vapour, that hung lightly, like a scarf, over the snowy peaks of the distant mountains.

As we watched this lovely shade, the sun sank below the horizon, a blaze of golden light shot up, the sea became deep purple, the snow-mountains gradually lost their rosy glow, and an unearthly pallor—beautiful, yet awfully like death—stole gently over the long line of peaks, growing paler and paler, until at length darkness hid the shore from our sight.

CHAPTER XIII.
SOUKOUM.

The next morning it was discovered, to the vexation of all on board, that we had overshot our mark. A headland had been mistaken, and the yacht was some miles beyond Soukoum-Kalé. We had to work our way back again therefore, and it was mid-day before the anchor was dropped in the roadstead opposite the little town.

Navigation off this coast is very difficult. There are but few charts, and even these few are not correct. Indeed it is hinted that there is no desire that the difficulties should be diminished.

The country around Soukoum is quite as beautiful as any we have yet seen; but the town itself, though its low, white houses scattered along the shore and up the sides of the wooded hills are picturesque enough, seems a small, insignificant place, little more than a Russian fort.

A Russian transport and three small ships of war were anchored near us, the decks and yards thronged with people anxious to see such an unusual, such a wonderful sight as an English yacht. The *Claymore* has the honour of being the first vessel to fly the Royal Yacht Squadron flag at Soukoum-Kalé.

On shore the same excitement prevailed. The beach was crowded with people, who watched our movements with the greatest interest and curiosity, evidently brought to a culminating point when they saw ladies and children on board. The English consul, Mr. D——, soon arrived, kindly anxious to give every assistance. By-and-by the governor and admiral, attended by their aides-de-camp, also came on board; and after a time we went on shore with them.

The beach where we landed was crowded with Russians and Circassians, many of the latter the wildest-looking creatures imaginable. They were mostly however fine, tall men, with remarkably erect and graceful figures, intelligent faces, and large, dark, fiery eyes. Their dignified bearing was in marked contrast to the depressed appearance and careworn countenances of the majority of the Russians.

In poverty and in rags a Circassian retains his independent, self-relying manner, and looks (what he generally is) a bold mountaineer, who, notwithstanding his nominal submission to a foreign power, preserves his liberty, and, with gun and sword, can defend his own against the world. This same gun and sword, it is asserted, are not unfrequently turned to other and less legitimate uses, for their owner does not scruple to avail himself of any favourable opportunity of enriching his purse by their aid.

The Circassian dress is very picturesque. Large, loose trousers are tucked into high boots, with a dark coat made full in the skirts, whilst across the chest is a row of long, narrow pouches, in which the ammunition is carried. The high cap is made of coarse cloth, the lower part covered with sheepskin. The horsemen from the mountains wear, instead of this cap, a long pointed hood, called a "papack," made of canvas and shaped like a monk's cowl, with two long ends that hang over the shoulders. Each man carries a carbine, rolled in sheepskin, slung at his back, and has pistols (often handsomely mounted in silver) stuck into his girdle.

Circassians, as a rule, have singularly small hands and feet, and the beauty of the latter is much enhanced by the boots they wear. These boots are made without soles, and are of scarlet or crimson leather so well prepared, and so fine in texture, that they at once take the shape of the foot, and fit like gloves.

The houses in Soukoum are low, being seldom more than one storey high; but they are very pretty, being generally surrounded by broad verandahs that are covered with creepers, and having gardens full of flowering trees and shrubs.

About the middle of the town, or village, is a large rough square, the exercising-ground of the troops; and beyond this again, bordered by a double row of trees, is a sort of road called by the dignified name of the Boulevard. All the best houses are here, including those of the governor and admiral. There may have been eight or ten more of nearly equal size. The others were very small, containing but two, or perhaps three rooms.

The road was exceedingly pretty, with its fine trees; and a raised pathway under their shade made a very pleasant walk. It led to a rough common, where several large flocks of geese were disporting themselves in the little clear pools of water.

For some reason or other,—why we never clearly understood,—Russians have an idea that the goose is the pet bird of all English homesteads, and that a flock of geese has a romantic charm to the English eye far beyond that which any other bird can possess. These geese were, therefore, pointed out to us by our companions as likely to awake many tender reminiscences of home. But it is a sad and, perhaps also, a humiliating confession to make, that instead of contemplating these excellent birds with feelings of tenderness, as suggestive of home nooks and corners in dear Old England, we gazed upon them with sentiments of the lowest and most earthly domestic interest. A tolerably long course of skinny chickens and preserved meats had so deteriorated our higher tastes and sensibilities, and had so sharpened our appetites, that the first thought was that now we would have roast goose for dinner, and that the excellent Domenico could replenish the empty poultry-coops.

But in truth the scene was very pretty, and wonderfully like England. The heathy common, with its patches of gorse and tufts of "bracken," the white cottages peeping out amidst the trees, the groups of birch and alder bushes that skirted the little pools, the clumps of rugged old Scotch firs, made us feel for a moment that we must have been seated on Prince Hussein's magic carpet, and in the twinkling of an eye had been transported to a sunny glade in the Hampshire New Forest. But ere the thought found words, a herd of buffaloes crossing the path, and then a group of wild figures armed to the teeth, their dark eyes glittering fiercely from beneath their white hoods as they dashed rapidly by, speedily dispelled the illusion, and showed how far we were from the peaceful highways and byways of home.

In a beautiful nook on the slope of a hill is a charming little house, a perfect bower of roses. This is the English consulate, and as far as the desires of the eye can be gratified, man could not wish for anything more lovely; but Mr. D——, as well as most people here, has been suffering acutely from fever.

The very beauty we admire, namely, the wondrous luxuriance of the vegetation, is one of the great evils of the country, or rather becomes so, from the carelessness and indolence of man. Were the land properly cultivated, Abasia (as this part of Circassia is called) would be a paradise. The soil is so fertile, and the climate so temperate, that nearly every description of grain, fruit, and vegetable might be grown with very little trouble.

It seems almost incredible that in a country so rich and productive that a few hours' industry would insure an abundant harvest, *every* fruit and vegetable, including even potatoes, should be imported from Trebisonde.

Unhappily the Circassians are too proud and too indolent to work, and until better guarantees can be given for the preservation of life and property, colonists cannot of course be expected to settle.

At present the Russian soldiers are the only agricultural labourers, and as their military duties are severe, the result is that only sufficient ground is cultivated to supply the horses with hay and forage.

Military service in the Caucasus has been for many years unpopular amongst the Russian regiments. The duty is arduous, and the great distance from the capital causes it to be looked upon, especially by the officers, as a banishment little inferior to that of being sent to serve in Siberia. Indeed, some of those we knew were of opinion the northern was the less objectionable station of the two, for the constant attacks of fever, from which it seems almost impossible to escape, cause, not only exhaustion of body, but a mental depression that is very trying to the sufferers.

This accounted for the haggard and cadaverous appearance of so large a proportion of the soldiery. We hear also that the ratio of mortality is very large. Fever prevails all the summer, and is more or less dangerous according to the quantity of rain that falls, but during the months of July and August it usually rages with frightful severity. During a rainy season the mortality is quite terrible.

Last year out of five thousand soldiers three thousand were suffering from fever, while there was not one case amongst the seamen on board the Russian men-of-war lying at anchor opposite the town.

Vessels, during the summer months, remain as far away in the roadstead as possible, the air from the town being so fraught with disease.

During the course of our walk we ascended a little detached hill called the Upper Fort, and felt immediately the relief of being able to breathe the fresh invigorating mountain breeze, after the relaxing warmth and dampness of the air in the town below. Happily the hospitals are here, for it is the only really healthy spot in Soukoum. Were the sick obliged to remain in the valley, the deaths would probably be doubled.

Close to the fort is a small house where Omar Pasha lived with some of his wives when the Turkish army occupied Abasia. It is quite a tiny place, only containing four rooms, but notwithstanding the confined space, the poor women, it is said, were never allowed to go out. Tradition, however, does not say whether their beauty was so dazzling that it was not safe to risk their being seen by the profane eyes of unbelieving Giaours.

The views on all sides were most lovely, but the very beauty had an air of desolate grandeur that produced a feeling of depression. A perfect network of steep narrow valleys extended beyond the region of wooded hills immediately before us. Great banks of forest clothed their steep sides, stretching far away, dark and silent, until their gloomy outlines were lost in the shadowy recesses of the mountains. Here and there the silver line of a distant water-fall caught the rays of the setting sun, and glittered for a few minutes amidst the sombre masses of the woods; but, though so near the town, no sound broke the stillness—no song of birds, no voice of man, no cheerful token of the neighbourhood of cattle or home life disturbed the silence of evening.

We had followed a sort of track that skirted the nearest valley. Wild flowers grew around in such beauty and profusion that it was impossible not to gather handfuls as we passed. Honeysuckle and eglantine hung in garlands from every bush; wild hops and vines festooned the trees. In every rocky hollow were tufts of the pretty caper-plant, with its lovely blossoms of mauve and white, while the ground seemed covered with bright geraniums, many-tinted asters, late cyclamen, and the dwarf myrtle. And then the wondrous beauty of the mossy wood we entered next, where the sunbeams quivered over a perfect carpet of lovely grasses, lichens, and graceful ferns. Charming though it was, we dared not prolong our stroll, for the sun was sinking low, and not only is the evening air supposed to be laden with fever, but our companions assured us that it would be scarcely prudent to be beyond the fort when night had come. We quickened our steps, but notwithstanding all our haste, it was nearly dusk before we arrived at the town.

It was startling to see, from time to time, a wild horseman gallop by, looking all the more wild and eerie from the dim uncertain light. Mounted on little wiry horses, they rode at headlong speed towards the gloomy passes in the mountains, and long after they were out of sight we could hear their swords clattering against their large stirrups as they dashed rapidly over the rough ground.

It is difficult to find adequate words in which to express our sense of the great kindness of all our friends in Soukoum. Not only have horses and an escort of Cossacks been placed at our disposal during the whole of our stay, but every little wish has been anticipated. As to our poultry coops, they have been filled to overflowing with the best poultry the place can produce, and the milk of the only available cow in the town has been devoted to our use. The wish of seeing the various ferns and wild flowers of the country speedily brought baskets of the most lovely specimens on board the yacht. Music and sketches were also among the generous gifts. In short, so great has been the kindness, that words fail with which to describe it.

Should, however, these few pages be ever seen by any of the kind and accomplished friends who made Circassia even a more enchanting land to us than we had pictured it in our dreams, they will see that they are remembered with feelings of the truest gratitude and admiration by their English guests.

Few people are more accomplished than the Russians; and in this remote corner of the world we have had musical evenings that would have obtained approval from the most fastidious connoisseur.

Beethoven and Chopin probably little thought their delicious melodies would beguile many a weary hour in countries beyond the Black Sea.

The Governor arranged, soon after our arrival, to take us a long ride towards the mountains, and on landing at the appointed hour we found General B—— awaiting us with quite a troop of men and horses drawn up on the beach.

Besides the horses provided for us, others had been prepared for Domenico and Mr. D——'s servant, who, under the guidance and protection of four soldiers, were to go on a foraging expedition to a neighbouring village. Domenico, as we have said, has many excellent qualities, but courage is not perhaps his most brilliant virtue. At the last moment his small amount of valour failed him. He entreated with such a rueful countenance to be allowed to go with our stronger party—with earnest gesticulations and in a torrent of Neapolitan he drew so moving a picture of what *our* feelings would be if he were brought back dead instead of the chickens—that our hearts were moved, and it was settled that he and the other servant should accompany us, and take the chance of what good luck might send in the shape of geese and turkeys.

The escort consisted of six Cossacks and a corporal. All were well armed with muskets, pistols, &c., but the horses they rode were so thin, and seemed so out of condition, that we wondered at first how the poor things could stand.

We had not long started, however, before we perceived that they *went* wonderfully well, and actually looked better at the end of the ride than they did at the beginning.

The horses provided for us were beautiful little Persian Arabs, lively yet gentle, perfectly free from vice, and having a light springy action most delightful to their riders. General B—— had bought them in Persia, and had paid a large price for them even there.

The guide, a young Circassian, grandly arrayed in a brilliant yellow coat and scarlet boots, and fully armed with matchlock, pistols, and sabre, rode at the head of the troop.

Circassian saddles look exceedingly clumsy and uncomfortable. They are very peaked and very high, but the Circassians are first-rate horsemen; they use short stirrups, have the regular English hunting-seat, holding on by the knees, and rise in their trot in a very unmilitary but thoroughly jockey-like fashion.

We had our own saddles, and they evidently excited much wonder amongst the little crowd that had collected. We were watched with absorbed interest, as the various preparations of tightening girths, &c., were made, but when at last Mr. Harvey mounted my sister and myself in the English fashion, the feelings of the spectators found vent in a little cry of astonishment.

We were deeply impressed with the warlike fashion of our departure. The guide and two Cossacks rode in front, then came General B——, some Russian officers, and ourselves, followed by the rest of the soldiers, and a formidable jingling and clattering there was as the little troop swept through the town.

We crossed the common, and entered a very pretty wood of beech and oak trees. Occasional openings showed the sea on one side, and on the other low, steep, wooded hills, with huge boulders of granite rearing their grey sides above the trees.

Some of the masses of rock were so smooth and round that they looked like gigantic marbles, as if the Titans had been disporting themselves amidst the lofty summits of El-Barouz, and had rolled some of their playthings into the valleys beneath.

From time to time we passed long narrow glens that gave vistas of apparently endless chains of hill and mountain; the nearest looking dark purple in the strong light, others beyond growing gradually paler and less distinct, until they became at last blended with the blue distance, a faint glimmer of snow alone indicating the most distant peaks.

As the day wore on a soft breeze arose, that just rustled the leaves and made the air fresh and cool, doubly refreshing after the great heat of the morning. The earth gave forth the sweet scent that so often comes after heavy dew. The grassy way was good; our horses were excellent. It was delightful to be once more on horseback—a pleasure we had not had for months; so, giving the rein to our willing steeds, on we went at a pace that evidently astonished the Cossacks, and delighted kind General B—— and our Circassian. As for the latter he was fairly enchanted; he waved his arms above his head, rose in his stirrups, and bending over his horse's neck, dashed forward at full speed.

This rapid pace, however, could not be kept up after leaving the grassy plain, for we then entered the hill country, where forest and thick underwood made the way more difficult, and where treacherous bogs had to be skirted and sometimes traversed.

These bogs during the winter and spring are almost impassable. During the summer months they can be crossed in certain directions. In consequence of the late drought, they are just now unusually firm, but nevertheless we had to jump over several little watercourses and dangerously green places.

Sometimes, too, the ground shook under the horses' feet as if it meant to swallow us up, but our sagacious animals made their way with the utmost precaution, and evidently thoroughly understood their business.

Very dreary-looking places were these bogs, as they lay brown and gloomy under the shadow of the forest, their treacherous surface only broken here and there by bushes of stunted birch-trees. We could well understand how goblin-like must seem the myriad lights of the will-o'-the-wisps, as they dance in unearthly fashion over such dark and dangerous morasses.

Again we plunged into the thick forest, and another hour's riding brought us to the entrance of a narrow defile, the gateway, as it were, to the mountain regions.

The way became rough and difficult, being merely the bed of a mountain torrent, and the number of loose and slippery stones made it very troublesome for the horses to find secure footing. The scenery grew wild and stern; great masses of rock hung over the pass, in many places almost meeting overhead.

Little streams came rushing down from the heights, tumbling headlong over the precipice, when they arrived at the steep walls of rocks that hemmed us in on every side.

The defile, or rather ravine, for it was evidently but a passage the stream had worn for itself in the course of countless ages of time, was so deep and narrow that it made one quite giddy to look up.

Vertigo ordinarily affects the head when looking *down*; we had never known the sensation before when looking *up* at a great height; but the rapid passage of the clouds across the narrow, crooked opening above, when looked at for a few minutes, made everything seem to whirl round.

Wherever a few broken stones had allowed a little earth to collect, masses of rhododendrons and groups of birch had taken root. Their graceful forms and bright green leaves made cheerful spots of life and beauty amidst the rugged severity of the gloomy scene.

As we advanced further into the pass, not a sound was heard but the rush of the mountain torrents, and the harsh cry of an eagle as he wheeled slowly over our heads.

We all became silent. It was almost disagreeable to hear the champing of the horses, and the occasional rattle of the accoutrements, as we moved slowly but steadily on, our companions keeping a wary look-out on all sides, though it was believed that the country was at present unusually quiet.

Still a very few more miles must be our limit. It would not be prudent to advance much farther into the wild region before us.

It must be admitted that on first starting we had thought our warlike escort was more for honour than for real use, but even before we had entered this savage defile it was evident how well it was for us that we were surrounded by so many brave protectors. "Prevention is better than cure," and a strong party often prevents an attack being made.

Once amidst the gloomy defiles and dark recesses of these wild mountains defenceless travellers would have no chance against a predatory band; they would be as sheep walking into a lion's den.

From time to time we had met parties of mountaineers, some on horseback, some on foot, but all completely and heavily armed.

Although in actual distance so few versts from the town, the mountains surround it so closely—the country is so desolate, and also intersected even in the lowlands by ravines and morasses—that, had we been alone, resistance to these armed bands would have been hopeless.

Before assistance could have arrived we should, in all probability, have been conveyed away to some distant fortress, there to remain until the required ransom had been paid.

The astonishment of the Circassians to see women riding in the European fashion was most amusing. Native women, when they travel, ride like men. It was evidently a deep mystery to them how we continued to keep on. They generally pulled up and watched us as long as we remained in sight, expecting, probably hoping, we should ere long fall off.

One man was so absorbed in wonder that he lost his seat. His horse made a sudden jump, and the rider fell so heavily, and with such a crash, that we thought he must be killed. However, in a few seconds, to our great relief, he jumped up, looking very crest-fallen (for such an accident is accounted exceedingly disgraceful), and climbed into his saddle amidst the jeers and laughter of his companions.

It may easily be supposed how delightful and interesting we found the ride. But pleasures must come to an end; days are short in these parts; evening was coming on, and it would be risking too much to let darkness find us on such dangerous ground.

Unwillingly, therefore, we had to content ourselves with longing glances at the wild ravines that branched upwards in all directions. The solitude, the gloom, the inexpressible grandeur of the dark frowning rocks, the very danger, gave an additional charm, and, like true women, we longed the more to penetrate into the forbidden land.

Fortunately we were all too much accustomed to mountain travelling to feel nervous when traversing narrow and lofty ledges, for it was decided that it would be more prudent to avoid the pass by which we had entered, and so regain the town by a different route. Our guide, therefore, led us up the face of a precipice by a pathway that looked only fit for goats, but the clever little horses made their way with a steadiness and skill beyond praise, and of which all the cavalcade could not boast, for at one or two uncommonly skeary places poor Domenico lost heart and dismounted, preferring to trust to his own powers of climbing, a very unwise proceeding on his part, for a horse will often make his way safely where a man's nerve may completely fail him.

We found it better not to look down too much. When we were occasionally able to do so, the savage wildness of the scene was inexpressibly grand, especially at one point where, on turning sharply round the shoulder of an almost perpendicular rock, we found ourselves hanging as it were over a chasm black as night itself, and where, at an immense depth beneath, we could hear the roar and chafing of waters, though the torrent itself was invisible in the darkness of the depth below.

Slowly and carefully we made our way down the steep side of the ravine, until we arrived at the bed of the stream that was to serve as road to take us back into the hill country. At this season the brown, turbid current, though it roared angrily over the many rocks and stones that impeded its course, was not deep, and, after the slipping and climbing we had had for the last hour, it was quite pleasant only to have to wade through water, notwithstanding the occasional splashings that it entailed.

This gorge was quite as narrow as that by which we had entered, and on emerging from its darkness and gloom into the brightness and verdure of the hills, we felt as Dante must have done when he returned to earth from his visit to the Inferno.

The stream partook of the character of the scene, and soon after entering the grassy plains and verdant woods became a pretty rippling river, though the masses of stones on each side its bed showed that its violence could be again excited by the winter rains.

A few versts from the town, on a steep grass bank, shaded by a picturesque group of beech, was a very pretty wooden house (the only habitation we had seen all day), something like a large Swiss *chalet*. The mother and family of the late Prince Dimitri Sherwasidzi, who died a few months ago, live here. The ladies, dressed in deep mourning, were sitting in the broad verandah. They wore black woollen robes, and had veils of the same sombre material wrapped round their heads. The dress was most funereal. The tall, slender women, with their gloomy drapery, that hung around them in heavy but graceful folds, looked like figures from a Greek frieze. Mourning here is very rigid. For three months after the death of the head of a family, the ladies see no visitors excepting near relatives. Every week the Princess Sherwasidzi, attended by her women, visits the grave of her son. For several hours they weep and mourn, casting ashes upon their heads with lamentable cries and screams.

Standing a little apart from the family dwelling is another similar but smaller house, entirely devoted to the entertainment of guests. Hospitality is much esteemed and largely practised by the upper class of Circassians. No greater praise can be awarded than to say that a man "keeps forty tables."

The ride back in the cool evening was very pleasant, but devoid of incident, with the exception of seeing our poor Domenico sent flying over his horse's head. After having so well surmounted all the little difficulties of the day, his horse stumbled over a sand hillock, and this inglorious somersault was the result. Happily no harm was done beyond a torn coat, but the Cossacks were immensely delighted at his discomfiture. Even the grim old corporal gave his grey moustache a pull to hide the unwonted smile in which he indulged.

CHAPTER XIV.
CIRCASSIAN MEN AND WOMEN.

Our life here is full of quaint contrasts—a curious mixture of wildness and civilisation. The days are passed in wild rides amidst the hills and mountains, the dash of danger that attends them adding zest to the interest of seeing scenery, magnificent in the sublimity of its savage grandeur, and exquisitely lovely in the tender beauty of its sequestered valleys and fern-clad forests.

At eight o'clock the scene changes, and we find ourselves in the midst of a most kind and agreeable little society, where music and dancing and merry talk make the hours pass much too quickly. The little world of Soukoum is of course very limited, but it comprises so many charming and clever people that one cannot help regretting that some of them should, like the flowers in the desert, be destined to bloom so far away from the more frequented haunts of men.

General B——, the Governor, is unmarried, but the Admiral's young wife, Madame G——, aided by her pretty sister, Mlle. Olga J——, contrives to make her rough Circassian house as attractive as if it were in Paris or St. Petersburg.

Mr. D—— is an excellent musician, and Count S——'s mazurkas and valses are so brilliant that a dancing spirit invariably comes upon all who hear them. Then there is a doctor, the merriest of men, who plays heartrending melodies upon the flute. Unluckily, however, in the midst of the plaintive death-strains of Edgardo and Desdemona, we catch sight of the brightest pair of little black Tartar eyes, twinkling with such a droll expression over the music, that instead of crying we all begin to laugh, which, it must be admitted, spoils the effect the musician intended to produce.

Last, though not least amongst our kind and charming friends, is the Princess Constantine S——, a young Russian from Moscow, who has lately married the brother of the reigning Prince of Abasia. Very young, very pretty, and accustomed to the luxuries and gaieties of a capital, she has accepted the difficulties of her life here with a good sense and with a sweetness of temper that have already done wonders in her Circassian household.

The Prince was, unfortunately for us, with his brother at Shamshesherai during our stay at Soukoum, but the friendly, even affectionate hospitality we received from Princess Constantine and her family, while it gave increased charm to our visit, added much to the pain we felt when the time came for saying the cruel word, "farewell."

How often we have thought since of the merry hours we spent together in that barn-like house. Though pretty outside, from the climbing plants and fine trees by which it was shaded, it would be difficult to find anything more comfortless than the interior. Great bare rooms, without ceilings, and where the rats sometimes run across the rafters, a general untidiness, and often also a want of cleanliness, make Circassian houses, though the owners may be very wealthy, anything but inviting to a foreigner. Princess Constantine and her mother had effected many improvements, especially with regard to cleanliness and order, but still the aspect of her home was cheerless in the extreme.

The salon was a large, whitewashed room, containing a table, a couple of sofas, and a few chairs that seemed to add to the dreariness of the long wall against which they were arranged; but there was a good piano, though unhappily it had occasionally to serve as sideboard and as a stand for several books.

The Princess's bedroom was somewhat more furnished, though scarcely more comfortable. The wooden planks of which the walls were made let in the wind through every joint, so that immense Persian rugs were stretched round the bed to keep off the intrusive breezes.

The dressing-table was like an oasis in the desert, so gay was it with lace and muslin; its grand gold toilette-service and looking-glass, set with rubies, seeming quite out of place in so comfortless an apartment.

The walls were hung with the Prince's magnificent arms and accoutrements. Some of the high-peaked Abasian saddles were very gorgeous, being covered with crimson velvet embroidered with gold. The arms would have excited the envy of many a Parisian "elegant," so fine was the temper of the sword-blades and daggers, and so beautiful were the jewelled hilts and scabbards.

The poor Princess gave a half-melancholy, half-ludicrous account of her first arrival from Moscow, and of her despair at the poverty-stricken, desolate appearance of her new home.

She has by degrees succeeded in introducing a little more order and comfort in the household, and hopes some day to have furniture; but in the present unsettled state of affairs, it is thought more prudent to avoid anything like display or expense.

She tells us that her brother-in-law, Prince Michael, who, besides being very rich, has also a salary from Russia as Governor of Abasia, keeps up a considerable amount of state at Shamshesherai.

The ladies of the family, though nominally Christians, retain nevertheless many of their Mohammedan customs. They never appear in public unveiled, and though allowed to see their male relatives, they lead a very secluded life, apart from the men, passing their time in smoking, making sweetmeats, and arranging their dresses. They receive little or no education, and speak neither Russ nor any other European language.

Our friend tells us that although very great beauties are sometimes seen, yet in her opinion Circassian women are not generally good-looking, and that the Abasians are decidedly plain. Certainly at present we have not seen one native woman with any claims to beauty.

The national dress, also, does not heighten their charms. They usually wear loose Turkish trousers, made of white cotton, and a peculiarly frightful upper garment of some dark cloth, made precisely like the coats worn by High Church clergymen—tight and straight, and buttoned from the throat to the feet. A striped shawl is sometimes twisted round them like an apron. A blue gauze veil is thrown over the head, and their hair, which is generally long and thick, is worn in two heavy plaits that hang down behind.

The beauties who obtain such great reputation in Constantinople and the West almost invariably come from Georgia and the valleys near El-Barouz. In those districts the women have magnificent eyes and fair complexions.

It must be admitted, also, that we have arrived too late in the season to see the good-looking girls. In short, they have all been sold.

Early in the year certain traders arrive from time to time, and it is rumoured that Circassian parents do not object to dispose of their daughters for a consideration. It is said also that the fair damsels themselves, far from making difficulties, are delighted to escape from the tedium of home-life, and to take their chance of being purchased by a rich pasha.

Although Prince Constantine's house was so badly furnished, so devoid of ordinary comforts, still there was a sort of Eastern grandeur in the multitude of servants and retainers who were attached to the household.

Land here is almost valueless, for Nature is so bountiful that her wild fruits, and a little Indian corn, with the addition of poultry that seem to feed and take care of themselves, amply suffice for the support of the inhabitants.

A great man's wealth is, therefore, estimated by the number of serfs he possesses, rather than by the extent of his territory.

The serfs are bound to supply their lord with a certain quantity of wood, poultry, and service, the latter duty being generally compounded for by one of the family becoming a permanent servant or workman in the household of their prince. The lord, on his side, bestows land and protection on his retainers.

Serfdom is not so galling here as it was in Russia, for the owner has no power, or at any rate it is not the custom, to sell his serfs; he may remove them from one part of his property to another, but even such a measure would be considered tyrannical.

In fact, serfdom in Circassia very much resembles clanship as it was in old times in Scotland. Each man is proud of his connection with his chief, and the chief considers himself bound to protect and avenge the wrongs of his followers.

Like the old Scottish chieftains, also, the Circassian princes, though possessing numerous bodies of retainers, and often vast tracts of country, are but scantily supplied with coin, and have but little means at their disposal for the due education of their sons, or for enabling them to obtain the cultivation of mind, as well as manners, that can be gained by seeing other countries.

From time to time the Emperor summons some of the young men to St. Petersburg. They there receive a certain amount of training and education, but like most half-civilised people, the young princes are, with few exceptions, so devoted to the wild life they have been accustomed to lead amidst their native mountains, that going to St. Petersburg is by no means popular.

Perhaps, also, it is considered but as another name for banishment; for occasionally, when the reigning family is supposed to be too influential, pretexts have easily been found for retaining the young heirs at the Russian Court.

The Prince of M—— and his mother have thus been for years in Russia, in spite of all their efforts to obtain permission to return to their own country. They remain in a sort of honourable captivity, receiving a large pension, while their estates at home are managed by the Russian Government.

The Princess, we were told, is a woman of remarkable talent and of very enlightened views. By her judicious measures she had effected considerable improvement amongst her people, but, unhappily for her, she was some years ago suspected, or accused, of corresponding with Schamyl, and was therefore at once removed from temptation. Her palace and gardens were at one time renowned for their beauty, but during the occupation of the country by the Turks, the palace was plundered and the gardens were destroyed, though Omar Pasha did his best to save them.

The invading army was on the whole harmless compared with the lawless bands of camp-followers, who, hovering on the flanks and rear of the Turkish troops, ravaged the unfortunate country, burning and destroying as they passed, when they found no more booty was to be obtained.

A few days after our arrival, we were painfully reminded of the insecurity of the country, by the intelligence that the body of a soldier had been found in the pretty valley we had crossed on our ride towards the mountains.

A party had been sent out to cut firewood; the unfortunate man strayed away from his comrades, and was missing when the detachment returned. His body was discovered this morning, shot through the head with a Circassian bullet. Though nominally in possession of the Russians, Circassia is still in a very disturbed state. The mountain fastnesses are held by the Circassians, and until roads are made, morasses drained, and the plains and valleys that lie between the mountains and the sea are inhabited and cultivated, predatory bands can traverse the country at their will, making it unsafe for any foreigner to venture beyond the protection of the Russian forts and pickets.

Even strangers can see that Circassia, like a lovely wild animal, must be tamed rather than beaten, and that roads and harbours will avail far more towards her complete subjection than the intimidating presence of a vast standing army.

Though the Abasians have now for some years been Russian subjects, their sympathies are with their highland brethren, and it is well known that they aid and abet the guerilla war that so incessantly harasses the district. The Russian officers declare that this species of hidden warfare is most trying to the troops. It brings neither honour nor profit, and the hatred that is felt by the Circassians is heartily returned by their conquerors.

In Georgia this ill-feeling does not exist. The people have shown themselves much more amenable to foreign rule. The Georgians are more indolent and less warlike than their neighbours in Circassia, and also have a great tie with Russia in being members of the same church.

The religion of the Circassians is shrouded in much mystery. Apparently they acknowledge no Supreme Being, they have no saints, nor do they observe any sacred days. Sometimes they sacrifice a chicken, though to whom, or for what, nobody knows. Some profess, however, a species of Mohammedanism, though they are absolutely disowned by all good Moslems, who consider such co-religionists a disgrace, and call them heretics and pagans of the worst description. They are amongst the few people in the world who make use of no sort of ceremony, even on occasion of a marriage. A certain price having been covenanted for, the father takes his daughter to her new home, and there leaves her, having received the gun, or horse, for which she is considered the fair equivalent. A mountain woman is valuable, as she is an excellent beast of burden, and a very hard-working slave.

From all we hear of the mountaineers, they seem to be a haughty, reserved people, proud of their poverty, of their unspotted lineage, and of their dauntless courage. Loving their wild country with passionate devotion, no reverses dishearten them. War is both their duty and their happiness, and at the cry of such a leader as Schamyl, they flock eagerly around his standard, prepared to suffer or to die in defence of their beloved prince, and of the wild liberty that is far dearer to them than life.

Few characters of modern days are invested with such romantic interest—nay, even at one time, with such mysterious interest—as that of Schamyl. Born in prosaic modern times, his life presents all the attributes of the hero of the middle ages. Endowed with personal beauty and strength rare even amongst the hardy tribe of which he was the chief, Nature had bestowed upon him another gift, yet more precious. She had given him the rare tact, the wondrous charm that wins personal love, and that enables men, and sometimes women, to rule mankind with absolute power. It is that love which makes men rush to death with heroic rapture, eager to shed their blood at the bidding of their beloved leader. The very faults also in Schamyl's character endeared him to his followers, or rather he adroitly contrived that they should be the means of binding his people still more closely to him.

Naturally of a morbid and melancholy disposition, he was at times subject to gusts of stormy passion that awed and subdued all those who witnessed the terrific bursts of rage which transformed the stern, calm man into a wrathful demon. Woe to him who aroused the dread spirit! The strongest men quailed before the furious glance, the mighty arm of their terrible chief. It is reasonable to suppose that these outbursts were but the effects of insanity, for during one attack of ferocious rage the unhappy man slew his young wife and infant child, to both of whom he had been tenderly attached. It is said that though in after-years many other wives filled his harem, never again did any woman gain that place in his heart which had been occupied by the young girl whom he had done to death with his own hand.

Not only did the great strength and wild fury of Schamyl awe his people into subjection, he skilfully led them to believe that on him the mantle of the Prophet had descended, and that in spirit he was constantly conveyed to the presence of the Almighty, there to receive the commands of the Divine Will. The wild ravings, therefore, that fell from his lips were treasured by his followers as direct communications from heaven.

Schamyl no doubt possessed sufficient control over himself to have some method in his madness, and contrived that his sentences should convey threats, encouragement, and orders calculated to strengthen his power amongst wild and independent people. It is difficult to ascertain, from the many conflicting statements, whether he was a Mohammedan or not; probably he found a certain amount of religious fervour of great utility in augmenting his influence amongst the more distant tribes, and he succeeded in making them believe in him as in a leader directly inspired by Heaven.

However visionary may have been Schamyl's claims to be a great prophet, there is no doubt that his talents as a soldier and as a politician were of a very high order.

The dark hour passed, who so thoughtful for his people—who so tender to his soldiers as this wild mountaineer? It is related of him that he often tended the wounded and sick with his own hand. He lived amidst his troops, sharing their privations and their danger, and was ever foremost in the fight. He rushed to the attack with a confidence that inspired his followers with unlimited faith, and for years it was believed that whenever Schamyl led in person victory was certain.

Besides this dauntless courage, all the Russian generals agree that he was a great and skilful strategist. Possessing a thorough knowledge of his native mountains, his positions were chosen with consummate judgment, and rarely did he make an attack unless fairly certain of the result. For years did he baffle the strong force and the renowned generals that Russia sent against him.

From his stronghold of Dargi-Vedenna, in Daghistan, he issued his mandates, which were carried out with unquestioning obedience by the devoted tribes.

At length time, unceasing attacks, and the tremendous power of money and strength began to tell. What could a few poor, brave, diminishing highland tribes do against the mighty Empire of All the Russias? The extent of Schamyl's dominions dwindled to the barren, bleak mountain sides in the heart of the Caucasus; but here his stronghold seemed impregnable, and but for treachery, perhaps, he might still be reigning in his wild mountain fortress. In an evil hour for him, he admitted to his friendship a foreigner, who basely betrayed the trust reposed in him, and, after months of starvation and suffering, the noble old warrior and the remains of his band were delivered over to captivity.

To the credit of the Russian Government, their prisoners were treated with the utmost kindness and consideration, and Schamyl has found a friend in the Czar, and a home at the Russian Court.

For the benefit of the country itself, it is greatly to be desired that Russia should speedily obtain possession of the whole of Circassia, and its adjacent provinces, but all the romantic sympathies of one's nature are stirred by the history of the few poor, brave men who fought to the death to preserve their liberty in their wild mountain homes.

Though the tribes who more immediately owned Schamyl's supremacy have been mainly destroyed, there are still many others who are as thorns in the sides of the Government.

The very fact of so distinguished a commander as General B—— being appointed to Soukoum is ominous of more than usual danger and difficulty. His presence denotes that there are grave apprehensions entertained that another desperate effort may be made by some of the most disaffected. It is earnestly to be hoped that the threatening storm may be averted in time. Such outbursts are most disastrous, and until they can be effectually checked no permanent improvement can be made in this lovely country.

Not only is General B—— a brave and distinguished soldier, he is a kind, generous-hearted man, and having passed the greater part of his life in the Caucasus, knows both the country and its many dialects thoroughly.

He has held several military commands, and has also been employed diplomatically both in Turkey and Persia, for he has the rare talent of speaking six Eastern languages, besides French, German, and Russ.

General B—— is by birth a Livonian, but has not seen his native country for nearly thirty years. He is now quite acclimated, and settled here, and not only have the wild beauties of his adopted home become very dear to him, but he also loves the stormy, adventurous life he leads. General B—— speaks in the highest terms of Prince Bariatinsky, who, he considers, has done more for Russia and for Russian interests in the last few years than any of the other commanders-in-chief have succeeded in doing for upwards of fifty.

Besides being an excellent soldier, the Prince is also a forbearing and judicious governor. The conciliatory measures he has adopted with the inhabitants of the conquered places have done much (especially in Georgia) towards establishing a friendly feeling between them and the Russian Government, and should this good understanding gain ground, and the distracted people once really know the blessings of peace, Russia may hope to see the country that has so long been merely a battle-field, costing treasures of blood and money, converted into a very mine of wealth, yielding abundance of corn and cattle from her rich valleys, and a mighty harvest of minerals from the vast storehouse of her mountains.

CHAPTER XV.
A LAST RIDE.

We endeavoured to return in a small way the kind hospitality of our friends by having a little *déjeûner* on board. Breakfast was prepared on deck, we arranged quantities of roses and ferns round the masts, and the yacht was dressed out gaily with all her flags. As the Governor came on board, the Russian ensign was hoisted at the fore, and when our friends left us, the *Claymore's* four little cannon fired a salute, with much military, or rather naval, precision.

The modest roar of our diminutive weapons had scarcely subsided when the huge guns of the Russian frigate bellowed forth the answering salute, then flash after flash came in rapid succession from the other vessels, until the air was filled with the warlike sounds. Long after the report was over, the distant thunder was heard muttering fainter and fainter as it rolled from cavern to cavern amongst the hills and valleys, as if it had awakened all the sleeping echoes of the mountains.

The more we see of this country, the more we are enraptured with its great and varied beauties. But beautiful as we find it now, every one tells us we can hardly form an idea of its loveliness when arrayed in its garment of spring flowers. Then the earth is carpeted with violets, narcissus, bluebells, cyclamen, and the many-coloured iris, while the sides of the hills glow with the red, pink, and lilac blossoms of rhododendrons and azaleas.

Wherever we walk and ride, we see the wild vine growing luxuriantly amongst the trees (its long branches often covered with fruit), making delicate green arches and canopies in the darker shade of the woods. The grapes are small, and not so sweet as when cultivated, but the slightly acid flavour is very agreeable in a hot climate. It is sad to see the bunches decaying on the vines, for the people never take the trouble of gathering them to dry for winter consumption.

Day by day the feeling of pain grows stronger to see that, while Nature has been so generous, so profuse in her valuable gifts, man will not even take the trouble to avail himself of the luxuries she offers with so lavish a hand.

Undeterred by the sad fate of the poor soldier, and confident in the valour of the gallant Cossacks and of the Russian officers who accompanied us, we made as many rides as possible in the neighbourhood of the town, but it was in vain to look with longing eyes towards the mountains. They were pronounced unsafe, and we dared not venture near them. Still the hilly low ground was so wondrously lovely that we could have ridden for months instead of days, and have found fresh beauties to charm us. The last ride we can never forget, perhaps because it had the sad charm of being the last—because we knew that each long lingering glance would never be renewed, that our eyes would never again rest upon the marvellous beauties of form and colouring that were lying in such abundant loveliness around us.

Soon after leaving the town we skirted a long narrow valley that gradually inclined towards the hills. We were riding through masses of fern, that began here and there to show a few bright autumnal tints. On the grassy slopes above and below were groups of magnificent trees, their long shadows almost stretching across the valley. Far away to the left the giant mountains reared their lofty heads, great dark lines marking the many ravines that scored their rugged sides.

So still was the air, so absolute was the hush of evening, that not a bush rustled, not a leaf moved in the great calm. We could only hear the tinkle of a little brook as it ran merrily amongst the brushwood beneath, and as we occasionally stopped to listen, there came the faint murmur of many a distant streamlet, as it threaded its way through the far away valleys and passes of the mountains.

The sun, that had been very oppressive before we entered the valley, now only glowed upon the tops of the hills, making the trees and rocks on one side quiver in the flood of light, while all was cool and fresh around us.

We pursued our way through fern and underwood, up hill and down, sometimes crossing the little stream that rippled with a thousand pleasant voices over shining stones and gravel, then again entering a thick wood, where the trees grew so closely together that the sunbeams in vain attempted to pierce the interlaced boughs above, and where we had to bend low over our horses' necks to avoid the masses of climbing plants that hung like ropes from the branches of the trees, until we arrived at an open space or plateau on the summit of a steep hill, and here we had a view as beautiful as it was extensive.

In this lovely region the atmosphere is so transparent that space seems almost annihilated. The eye travels far into the deep blue distance, tracing peak after peak in the wondrous clearness, until at length sky and mountain are blended into one line of quivering light, and the sight, fatigued with the magnitude and remoteness of objects on the vast horizon, seeks rest by gazing on the tender green of the fair valleys spread so invitingly around.

Far, far away, glittering with dazzling whiteness, was the range of mighty snow-mountains, some of the nearer peaks frowning majestically above the sombre masses of the great pine forests that stretch for more than a hundred miles into the interior of the country. The chain of the Caucasus is considerably more lofty than that of the Alps. The highest point of El-Barouz is rather more than 2,000 feet higher than Mont Blanc; but from the climate being so much warmer, there is apparently less eternal snow here than in Switzerland.

The valleys very much resemble those of the Tyrol, near Botzen. The same rich pastures, the same fertilizing streams, sunny slopes, and wooded hills are found here, but, unlike happy Tyrol, in the sister vales of Circassia not a house is to be found, and, unless a warlike band should pass, not a human being may be met with for hours.

During this day's ride the only man we saw was a goatherd, who, fully armed with sword and gun, was tending his flock of Circassian goats. These pretty creatures, smaller than those of Greece and Syria, are covered with long delicate hair, with which the Abasian women make many fine stuffs. The man was sitting under a tree up which a vine had climbed, and the ripe grapes were hanging in great clusters, high on the upper branches. Seeing that we looked both thirsty and tired, with the courtesy of a true gentleman and mountaineer, he threw down gun and sword, climbed the tree with the activity of a squirrel, and in a few minutes descended, laden with bunches of the lovely purple fruit, which he offered us with a grace of manner both simple and dignified. We had come into his native woods, and with the easy bearing of a stately host he offered his guests the best refreshment in his power. He then showed us his matchlock, of which he seemed not a little proud. It was made of beautifully-polished walnut wood, had scarcely any stock, and was so small that it looked like a pretty child's toy.

Like most mountaineers, the Circassians are excellent marksmen. They fire very quickly, so much so that they scarcely appear to take aim. On horseback they are equally at home, and load and fire with the greatest rapidity when at full gallop. War with them makes the delight as well as the occupation of their lives. They despise and avoid every sort of domestic and agricultural employment, and consider even hunting, unless in pursuit of some dangerous animal, beneath manly dignity.

To make the boys hardy and independent, as soon as they are old enough to sit on horseback they are sent to some friend's house, in order to be completely removed from the enervating influence of home. Here they remain several years, only occasionally visiting their parents. During this period they are taught warlike exercises, and are encouraged to encounter every description of danger and fatigue. Often are these hardy lads sent into the mountains during the severest winter weather to pass their days in the saddle, their only shelter at night a cave or an overhanging rock, their only food the roots of grasses and herbs.

No wonder that the Russians find it hard to subdue men who not only from their earliest youth have been thus inured to hardship, hunger, and thirst, but are also entrenched amidst the wildest of mountain fastnesses—fastnesses that can only be reached by many days' journey through forests and over morasses, where vegetation grows with such rank luxuriance that few would encounter willingly the dangerous miasma that reigns there nearly all the year.

Besides weaving woollen stuffs for clothing, the women of Abasia and Georgia make very pretty striped shawls and rugs from the long hair of the Circassian goat. They also excel in dyes, the colours mostly used, red and dark blue, being exceedingly fine in shade. The red is clear and brilliant, and the blue is quite free from the black dingy hue of the cloth worn by the Fellah women in Egypt, but is like a dark shade of the bright "Impératrice" blue. They also make the crimson boots or slippers that are worn alike by both sexes. The manufacture is very simple: the skins are scraped, tanned, and then dyed. The boots are cut out in a single piece and sewn up in front, the seam being lined with a narrow strip of leather. They are then thoroughly soaked in a mixture of resinous gum and water, which makes them nearly waterproof, and the owner should wear them thus wet for a few hours. The process is not very agreeable, but has its reward, inasmuch as the boots then take the exact shape of the feet, and fit with the pliability and comfort of a glove.

The women have besides a very ingenious way of carving beads. A long piece of wood, dyed red or black, is pierced lengthways by a heated wire. It is shaped either into an octagon, or is smoothed round. Then, with a knife and heated needles, it is cut and engraved into various patterns. Considerable taste is often shown in the designs, many of them being remarkably intricate and pretty. When the wand is sufficiently decorated, the beads are sliced off the size required. Beyond these primitive ornaments, we could not hear of any other *articles de luxe* being manufactured in Abasia.

In Georgia there are native jewellers, who make both gold and silver ornaments, and we saw some bracelets and necklaces made of gold that seemed very pure. The designs were also good, but the workmanship was coarse and ill-finished, and far inferior to the jewellery both of Persia and India.

But now the day had come when we must leave this fairy-like Eastern land—this earthly Paradise, where war, suffering, and trouble have taken such deep root. Perhaps, were it happy, peaceful, and prosperous, one would care for it less, for prosperity and riches have little need of sympathy, and can always ensure plenty of friends, whereas a poor people and a distracted country are thankful to accept all the friendship that may be bestowed upon them.

It may appear like exaggeration to say what real pain also it was to part from such newly-made friends, but we must have had very cold hearts not to have been touched by the great, unmerited kindness we had received. So now we must say good-bye to the joyous rides, to the merry evenings, that kindly intercourse has made so pleasant, and can only look forward, in exchange, to many a rough day and night on the stormy waves of the Black Sea.

As usual in this world, past pleasures must be paid for by some pain, and our visit here has been both so charming and so interesting, that we have been beguiled into making a stay somewhat longer than warranted by strict prudence.

Autumn brings many a storm to this easily-excited sea, and we shall be fortunate if we get back to the Bosphorus, or Sevastopol, without a "streak," as it is called, of bad weather. At present, however, all looks fair and sunny, the wind is favourable, to-night therefore we leave. Our friends accompanied us to the shore, and the last cordial hand-shake was given.

When we arrived on board the yacht we found that kind thoughts for us had already preceded us there. Flowers, grapes, music, drawings—everything they thought could add to our comfort or pleasure—had been sent on board by these kind people.

The anchor was up, the sails were set, the yacht was only lying-to until we embarked. The sea was as smooth as glass, the light of the rising moon covered the mountains with a tender veil, as we glided slowly away from Soukoum. Not a sound broke the silence of the night but the gentle wash of the water against the bows of the vessel. A soft breeze just filled the sails, and with really sad hearts we watched landmark after landmark disappear, until, on rounding the headland of the bay, the last light of the little town was shut out, and we said farewell, probably for ever, to the loveliest spot we have ever seen.

CHAPTER XVI.
SINOPE.

After leaving Soukoum we had three days of fine weather, though the winds had been somewhat capricious and baffling. Still we had done well, having had a run of 102 miles during the first twenty-four hours, and of 86 during the next; but on the 24th of September the wind began to moan ominously, and a thick fog was drawing up to windward like a curtain. The sea began to heave up and down with a sort of heavy, sullen motion, as if gathering its strength before a battle of the elements began.

Under these circumstances, and having a wish also to see Sinope, we resolved to go there, rather than brave the threatening gale. The helm was therefore put up, and about seven p.m. we made out one high and two low islands, which, on nearer approach, resolved themselves into a very narrow isthmus, that, stretching far away into the sea, terminated in a steep rocky promontory.

On the neck of the isthmus stands Sinope, commanding a beautiful view of the long range of mountains and wooded hills that line the coast. The town itself is a quaint place, tightly squeezed into some old castellated walls, with a fierce little pepper-box of a fort at each corner. Outside the town, a long straggling Greek suburb runs up the hill for a considerable distance, its low red and brown houses looking very picturesque amongst the groups of cypress and fig-trees. The roadstead, though open and exposed to the east, has the reputation of being perfectly secure, and we find ourselves in quite a little crowd of Greek, Turkish, Austrian, and Russian vessels. It seems, therefore, that others besides ourselves have had forebodings of bad weather, and have taken refuge in this, the only safe anchorage on the southern side of the Black Sea. It is singular, however, that the anchorage should be so safe, for it is difficult to believe that a heavy sea would not set into the bay, should the wind come from any quarter between north-east and south. It is said, however, that a vessel has never been known to be driven from her anchor; so the only solution is that these winds never blow here with violence. Certainly during our stay, though a tremendous sea was running about a mile or two out, but little swell ever came up to the anchorage.

On the morning after our arrival, an intimation came from the Pasha (one of the Sultan's numerous brothers-in-law), that he wished to pay us a visit. Soon after twelve his Highness arrived, attended by a very numerous suite, and accompanied by a Greek gentleman, the Austrian consul.

We were somewhat dismayed at the sight of such a goodly company, as our little cabins could not possibly accommodate so large a party of guests, and a Turk of high rank does not like to remain on deck. All were anxious to come below; it was therefore somewhat difficult to prevent undue crowding, for the Pasha was so interested in all he saw, that he insisted upon visiting every part of the vessel. He appeared an exceedingly intelligent man, and had a vivacity of manner somewhat unusual in a Turk.

When the cakes and sweetmeats appeared they were accompanied by champagne and liqueurs, both of which beverages were highly approved of. Happily by the laws of the Koran they are not considered wine, and the champagne was drunk in tumblers without any hesitation.

As the Governor descended into his state barge, manned by ten rowers in grand but rather dirty crimson jackets and fezzes, the yacht gave him the proper salute of fifteen guns, a compliment that was promptly returned by a Turkish man-of-war, to the intense joy of all the little boys in the town, who came flocking out of numberless narrow streets and alleys in an astonishing variety of dress, or rather undress.

Later in the day we proceeded to make a little tour round the town.

Sinope is divided into two parts, one inhabited by Turks, the other by Greeks.

The streets in the Greek quarter do not deserve the name. They are little better than rough water-courses, and are so narrow that the overhanging eaves of the houses almost touch each other. But what a wealth of picturesque beauty do these old houses present to the eye of an artist! Built entirely of wood, they are either painted a deep chocolate colour, or are left to brown and blacken with age, whilst so much shadow is lightened both by the great masses of moss or lichen that cling to the roof, and by the bright green of the vines that half cover the walls.

The mode of building is peculiar. The frame is joined together, and the roof is put on and finished. The walls are then made by means of layers of shingles (long narrow pieces of wood), fastened to the upright posts. These planks are of uneven length, and project over each other in a confused irregularity, which though charming in a sketch, leaves so many yawning crevices that each house must be a veritable temple of the winds.

The majority of the houses were much larger than might have been expected in so small and poor a town; but sometimes as many as ten or twelve families will live together, not in separate flats or apartments, but as one household.

It would seem as if in days of yore their ancestors must have been bitten by tarantulas, for dancing is a perfect mania with the Greeks here of all ages and classes. "Young men and maidens," old men and women, dance every evening, with an animation and an unwearied delight that neither poverty nor age seems able to diminish. Their principal aim, therefore, in building, is to have a large "salle de danse" for winter use, and as soon as this portion of the house is completed, the various families squeeze themselves into a few little rooms, contentedly enduring gaping walls and half-finished floors, so long as they have space for the beloved Romaika.

Though the houses are so crowded, they are nevertheless beautifully clean. A constant scrubbing seems going on, a process, strange to say, that is also extended to the inhabitants.

The women are really lovely, their features having the delicately cut outline that is so beautiful in the ancient Greek statues. Many have exquisitely fair complexions, and we fell in love immediately with their hair, for it had that dusky, half golden, half red tint only seen in the tresses of the gorgeous beauties of Titian and Georgione. It was a painful disenchantment to find that it owed its beauty not to nature, but to henna—in fact it was dyed. So enamoured are the Sinope women of this colour, that even the babies in arms have their scanty little locks tinged with the ruddy hue. Still, putting aside the disappointment of their hair, the women were worthy of all the admiration we bestowed upon them. Not only have they delicate features and complexions, but their eyes also are unusually beautiful; large, lustrous and dark, without being black, they have a tender, deprecating look that reminds one of the inexpressibly touching expression seen in the eyes of the unhappy Beatrice Cenci.

It is a well-known saying that pretty women generally dress well; either they adorn the dress, or the dress adorns them. The Sinope beauties are no exception to the rule, and the gay costume adds another attraction to the charms of the wearer.

On a fête-day a Sinope belle puts a many-coloured handkerchief over her head, which she ties as tightly as possible under the chin, in order to make her cheeks look round and smooth. In this, perhaps, she is a little mistaken, as ladies of other lands are who tighten their waists by way of improving their figures.

Another handkerchief is twisted round the head, beneath which the hair falls in two or three long thick plaits, while a few little curls are coquettishly allowed to stray over the forehead.

Her cloth jacket, of some bright colour, generally scarlet, blue, or green, is half covered with a rich embroidery of black or gold braid, and is left open in front, to show a full white chemise that is drawn up closely round the throat. A short petticoat of fringed silk, or a striped shawl of many colours is worn over large Turkish trousers, the toilet being completed by a crimson scarf fastened as a sash round the waist. Altogether it would be difficult to find a more brilliant or becoming costume.

The fair damsel also wears all her worldly wealth on her head and neck, and hanging from her ears, in the shape of long strings of gold or silver coins.

Unlike their Turkish neighbours, therefore, the Sinope Greeks have the inestimable advantage of being able to ascertain by the same glance whether the fortune equals the fair face of the young beauties amongst whom they have to select their wives.

For the first time for some years we saw again, not only middle-aged women, but women of a middle age, that were both well preserved and good-looking. In most countries the men have their proper allowance of the complete *seven ages*, but out of England, and in Eastern countries especially, it is rare to find women of the poorer classes who have more than three—namely, childhood, girlhood, and decrepit old age. From the second to the third is only a step, and a young girl has scarcely passed the bloom of early youth ere she changes in a marvellously short time into a wrinkled, toothless, shrivelled old woman. It was really refreshing to look at the good-looking women of *uncertain age* at Sinope; they had such a bright, matronly, and, if the simile may be used, such a sunshiny air about them.

The people seemed wonderfully good-natured, and bestowed upon us many nods and pleasant looks, as if they were really glad to see strangers in their little town.

Leaving the Greek quarter, we came to a broad, open space, with a few groups of cypress scattered about—the Turkish burial-ground, chosen with much taste, as is usually the case with Turkish cemeteries. Placed on the narrowest part of the isthmus that unites the promontory to the mainland, it commands lovely views over both bays.

We crossed a shaky draw-bridge, and, passing under an old mouldering gateway, found ourselves in the Turkish town—in the real region of true believers—not modern Turks, such as are now mostly seen in Constantinople, in Frank dresses and polished boots, but amongst grave, old-fashioned Moslems, arrayed in the flowing robes and large decorous turbans of days gone by.

The women, not nominally veiled in transparent and becoming clouds of muslin, but closely wrapped in sheets of such uncompromising calico that not even the tip of a nose could be seen, glided about like spectres, occasionally stopping under the shadow of a wall, to peep curiously at the unwonted spectacle of Christian women passing through their streets.

Finding ourselves in such an assemblage of "The Faithful," I became suddenly conscience-stricken on account of my cambric morning gown, which was really very pretty, but unhappily of a delicate *green*!! We could not but see the angry glances cast on the objectionable shade, so, although the evening was very oppressive, I hastened to hide myself as much as possible under the folds of a large shawl, doing my best, therefore, to prevent the scandal of the sacred colour being seen on an unbelieving "Giaour."

Dried fish and tobacco seemed the staple commodities of the place, and in spite of the exceeding cleanliness both of houses and people, they cause an ancient and fish-like odour to linger in the streets.

Leaving the town by a gate opposite to that by which we had entered, we found ourselves on the sea-shore. The big waves came tumbling in on the beach in great angry masses, and as they poured back again with a sullen roar, the old walls of the town seemed to quiver to their foundations, as if many more high tides and stormy seas would speedily lay them low. But old and tottering as they appear, they have for nearly three centuries resisted the efforts of their enemy, and the waves, by their own violence, have helped to make a little sand-bank that now seems to protect the ancient walls from their too near approach. The air was heavy and oppressive, giving that sensation of nervous foreboding that so often precedes physical or mental trouble. A long line of lurid clouds showed where the sun had gone down with angry redness, and some very dark streaks on the grey waters at the horizon seemed to say that to-morrow's rising would be as stormy as to-night's farewell.

The Austrian consul tells us that for some years *the* storm of the year has always taken place during the last week in September, the 26th being an especially fatal day. That luckless period is now over, so we venture to hope that the muttering tempest may but be moving on its way to other seas.

Though the short twilight was scarcely over as we again crossed the Greek quarter, not a soul was to be seen—not a light glimmered at a window; every street was silent and deserted. After the customary dance the people of Sinope, like the birds, go to bed with the sun, and a feeling came over us as if we were guilty of some degree of *fastness*, almost of dissipation, in not also being at home and in bed, like other respectable people, though it was little past eight o'clock.

A few hours later the storm burst forth in good earnest, and raged all night with great fury. Towards morning the wind somewhat suddenly went down, but a tremendous sea was running beyond the roadstead.

Three large steamers put in soon after dawn. One of them close by us presents a really pitiable spectacle. There are between four and five hundred Persians on board, and the deck is a scene of dirt and wretchedness such as would be difficult to find equalled. The Persians will never separate from their luggage; they sit on their goods all day and sleep on them all night. During the heavy sea yesterday the waves washed completely over the vessel, drenching these miserable creatures as well as their goods. From the deck being so encumbered the water could not escape, and these wretched people were lying for hours as in a bath, and in a frightful state of prostration and suffering, the combined effects of terror and sea-sickness. Some of them are now trying to dry their rags in the occasional gleams of sunshine, and the ship is covered with sheep-skins, bits of old shawls, carpets, and the complicated articles of clothing only known to Eastern toilettes.

As we wished to see the country, the Governor kindly lent us horses, and, accompanied by the Austrian consul, we set out in the afternoon for a ride. To do us still more honour, the Pasha had also sent two of his body-guard to attend us. More villainous-looking individuals it would have been difficult to find anywhere. Our conviction was that they must have been, even if, as we hoped, they no longer were, part of a robber-band. In that case they would prove far more efficient protectors than any regular soldiers could be, as in all probability they kept up friendly intercourse with their old companions.

Edmond About, in that witty and entertaining work, "La Grèce Contemporaine," gives one of his most amusing and clever descriptions, when he represents the brigands and soldiers as being on such friendly terms with each other that they take turns in claiming the victory in the occasional little encounters that from time to time take place, in order to keep up appearances, amicably dividing the spoil when the affair is over.

After paying a visit to the consul's wife, a pretty little Venetian, with two bright-eyed children, we mounted our horses, and passing through the Greek suburb, descended the hill and turned towards the mainland.

Soon after leaving the town, the country becomes barren, though the soil itself seems rich, and would probably be exceedingly fertile if well cultivated. Here and there were a few patches of corn, but tobacco is the principal crop. Great bunches of the fragrant leaves were hanging up to dry, suspended from poles in the middle of the fields. The tobacco grown near the coast is considered remarkably good, so we resolved to make some purchases for the benefit of smoking friends at home, and bought a quantity of the very best the district could produce for five piastres an oke. As there are eight piastres in a shilling, and as an oke contains about two and a half English pounds, it is hardly necessary to say how cheap this was. The same tobacco costs in Constantinople from 70 to 100 piastres an oke. Under these circumstances it seems wonderful that a regular trade should not be established, but such is the inertness of the inhabitants that there is no direct communication either with the capital or with Odessa, only an occasional trader from time to time putting in here. There are no roads from the town into the interior; only sufficient tobacco, therefore, is grown to supply the neighbouring villages.

The country is undulating, and, cantering up a little slope, we found ourselves on the summit of the cliffs that project into the western bay. On three sides was the sea, on the fourth the magnificent chain of mountains that run from the coast far into the interior of Asia Minor.

The day was wild and stormy; the sea broke with a deep, hollow roar amongst the caverns of the rocks. Every now and then fierce gusts of wind drove the clouds madly across the sky, but over the mountains there lay a broad band of sunshine, lighting up the little upland pastures, and making the patches of bright green still more vivid in contrast with the dark shadow of the forests at their feet.

Riding along the cliffs we obtained an excellent view of the singular position of Sinope. Built on a narrow strip of land, scarcely a quarter of a mile broad, it commands the two bays, and overlooks for many miles the undulating plain that stretches from the coast to the foot of the mountains. In old times, when the town was fortified, it must have been impregnable, both from sea and land; now the old castellated walls are little more than ruins. One portion, the remains of an ancient tower, said to have been part of the Palace of Mithridates, is remarkably picturesque. The leafy branches of briers and hops now trail across its old brickwork, and the tendrils of the wild caper have clasped in tight embrace many a column and mass of sculptured marble that lies lowly on the ground.

Ever since we have been here, notwithstanding the kind assistance of both Pasha and consul, we have had the greatest difficulty in procuring meat, bread, or milk. We were surprised therefore to see outside the town patches of grass that would have afforded excellent pasturage both for sheep and cattle. But it seems, in respect of *cow* government, Sinope is a republic, every cow doing as seemeth good to herself. She goes out in the morning when she likes, if in the evening it is borne on her mind that she would like to be milked, she comes home, but should her maternal feelings be weak, or should she wish to call upon her friends at a distance, she does not return for a day or two. Under these circumstances the supply of milk is precarious, and as to the bread, it is of the most primitive description. A coarse, dark-brown, nearly black meal is made into a paste by mixing it with a little water. It is then rolled into thin sheets about the size of a small round tea-table, and baked. When quite fresh this bread is not unpalatable, though fearfully indigestible, but the great drawback is that it is apt to get mouldy on the smallest provocation, and after it has been made a few days requires scraping and rebaking before it is possible to eat it.

Then, as to the butchers' meat, that is also a vain dream. There is a tradition that once there was a butcher's shop in the town, but this was in a time so long ago that even the oldest inhabitant does not remember it. However, we are told that perhaps some day we may get a wild boar, so we cheer ourselves with this hope, and try to think the unvarying chickens are not so very thin nor so very tough, after all.

CHAPTER XVII.
STORM-CLOUDS.

After blowing another hurricane all night there is this morning a decided improvement in the weather. The wind has gone down nearly as suddenly as it rose, though the sea is still running very high.

Some of the old wooden houses towards the outskirts of the town, where they were more exposed to the violence of the storm, have suffered considerable damage, and two have literally been blown down. Happily, the inhabitants were able to escape in time, and no lives have been lost.

As I was anxious to make some sketches before being prevented by our own departure, or by some of the prettiest houses tumbling into ruins, we went early on shore on a drawing expedition; but amongst so many picturesque spots, it was quite an *embarras de richesses* to know where to begin. At last I set to work upon a narrow street with dark-brown houses, whose overhanging eaves almost touched their opposite neighbours.

How I longed to have the skill of a really good artist, especially to draw one low projecting window which the leafy branches of a vine had formed into a little arch. A stray sunbeam was gleaming brightly on two fair young faces as they peeped shyly at the strangers through the framework of the tender green leaves. It was difficult to decide which shone brightest in the dark street, the bright eyes or the bright sunshine.

With this charming exception the place had seemed deserted when the sketch began, but after a few strokes had been made sundry little groups appeared at the doors, and emboldened by our pretending to take no notice, they gradually approached. Some of the older women ventured at last to look over my shoulder to see what I was about, and, when house after house appeared on the paper, their delight could no longer be controlled, and they eagerly called the owners to see the wonderful production.

Having accomplished the houses as well as I could, I wanted some figures to complete the little picture, and tried to sketch in as rapidly as possible a group of pretty girls who stood near. But this was going too far, and was too great a tax on their courage. They fled instantly; for so great is their dread of the *evil eye* that they, no doubt, felt persuaded that, were they to allow their likeness to be taken by a stranger, it would entail certain misery upon them. In southern countries one must carefully avoid noticing young people too much, and must especially beware of praising little children. A mother would think it most cruel *kindness*, as it would be directly casting the *jettatura* upon her child.

In many parts of Calabria (the stronghold of this superstition) it does not do for a friend, if a foreigner, to say a word even in favour of that generally-praised member of the family, the baby. Like the women of a Turkish harem, the children of a Christian household are too sacred to be mentioned.

Although they ran away, I was glad to find my Sinope friends were not irrevocably offended, for they turned up again when I began the next sketch. They gathered close round, evidently much interested in me and my doings, but though there was so much interest, there was not the least rudeness. It is to be feared that a strange artist, in a foreign costume, would not meet with such good-natured forbearance in an English village.

I was examined critically, however, and I could understand enough of what they were saying to know they were remarking upon my nose, eyes, mouth, hair, dress, &c. They were evidently much puzzled as to the use of the little hood belonging to my cloak, lifting it up, and making numerous interrogative signs; at last they arrived, I am certain, at the conclusion that it served to carry bread or babies in.

When the drawing was finished, a nice, fresh-looking old woman, a greater person probably than all the rest, as she wore some very large coins round her neck, came out of the crowd, seized my hand, kissed it several times, and then, tucking it tightly under her arm and pointing to the public baths close by, tried to pull me towards them. Whether she wished me to sketch them, or whether, in the excess of her good-will, she wished to present me to the rest of "the world of Sinope" (for in these parts the bath is the women's club, where they meet to drink coffee and sherbet, and talk over each other's affairs), must for ever remain a mystery, for though we both talked, we neither understood. She bowed persuasively, I bowed negatively, and clung tightly to my companion, for I was really afraid, from the excess of kind friendship, of being carried off against my will. At length, finding I was not to be moved either morally or physically, she again repeatedly kissed my hand, and with many smiles and friendly looks we parted.

We then strolled on as far as the Turkish burial-ground, enjoying the bright sunshine and the fresh air, for though so rough and stormy at sea, on shore it was very pleasant. Beyond the cemetery is an open common that extends to the edge of the cliffs that line the bay opposite to that where the yacht is lying.

Out at sea everything looked wild and desolate. Great leaden-coloured waves were beating in angry foam against the rocks; not a sail was to be seen; a few gulls were slowly flapping across the dreary waste of water, their hoarse cries sounding as if they too were uttering harsh warnings of coming disasters and death. But what a curious contrast as we turned from so eerie a scene and looked towards the town! On this side the sun was shining brightly, the birds were singing in the bushes close by, whilst several groups of Turkish women, seated under the cypress trees near the cemetery, made the scene gay with their many-coloured ferighies.

Turning inland, the day was so warm that we were glad to sit down on an old wall under the shade of a leafy fig-tree, though, when facing the sea, the keen, sharp wind had made us draw our cloaks closely round us. Such is essentially the climate of Sinope, summer and winter at the same time. No wonder, therefore, that the scourge of the place is consumption. The consul tells us that spring and autumn are nearly nominal seasons. The hot days of summer send the snow away, and when they again begin to decline rain and winter come together. The sun rules the temperature completely; when he shines the days are hot, even in mid-winter, and again in summer, should he withdraw his rays, and leave the sky gloomy and cloud-covered, there is a sudden chill in the air that is far more injurious to health than the actual cold of winter.

It was not until the 2nd of October that the weather cleared sufficiently to enable us to leave Sinope. Then, however, all promised well for a prosperous voyage. With a clear, blue sky, calm sea, and a fairly favourable breeze we set sail for the Bosphorus. For twenty-four hours the yacht dashed gaily along; and we were all merry with the anticipation of being speedily with our friends at Therapia, when a sudden change came over the sunny prospect. A little cloud, no bigger than a man's hand, was seen to windward. Though the sky was still blue, the sea calm, and the sun shining brightly, the glass went down with alarming rapidity. Suddenly the wind began to moan with a wild melancholy wail, a great darkness rapidly spread over sea and sky, except along the horizon; there a pallid streak of light showed where the storm was stalking on, lashing the sea into a perfect whirl of foam as it tore its way over the water. On came the squall with wondrous quickness. There was nothing to be done but to make the best of our way back to Sinope Bay, as it was evident that ugly weather was again threatening.

In less than an hour from the time when the little cloud had been first perceived the yacht was running before a heavy sea with scarcely a bit of canvas on her, but before night we rounded the promontory off Sinope, and were at once in smooth water.

Instead of returning, however, to our old anchorage, we put in to Ghirgeh, a little town on the other side of the bay, where, it was said, excellent shooting and good provisions were to be had. Unluckily, landing is a work of difficulty should there be any sea, or even swell, for there is a reef of rocks close to the shore that can only be crossed in tolerably smooth water.

The storm was not of long duration, though it was fierce while it lasted. It raged all night with much violence, but the following morning all things again looked propitious.

The breeze, though it blew rather fresh, was fair for the Bosphorus; we were getting impatient at so much delay. We might have remained days at Ghirgeh without being able to land, for with the wind from this quarter the surf beat heavily on the reef, and the boat that had been sent on shore in search of provisions had returned half full of water, with the men drenched to the skin.

Game and meat were also found to be "myths," and as the people on shore declared the gale was now well over, once again we set sail for Constantinople.

"Those who go down to the sea in ships, these men see the works of The Lord, and His wonders in the great deep."

We thank Him who stills the raging sea, that in His mercy He has guarded us through so fearful a tempest.

We had left Ghirgeh on Tuesday. Late on Wednesday afternoon once more the warning glass fell rapidly, and the breeze that had been fresh and steady suddenly dropped. Towards evening we were almost becalmed, little puffs of hot air only occasionally fanning us as the yacht rose slowly on the heaving sea. But about one o'clock that night, the gale came upon us with all its force, preceded by an icy wind that seemed to freeze the ropes into bits of iron.

No sooner was the roar of the mighty tempest heard across the waters than the sea, lashed into madness by the tremendous force of the wind, turned into a seething cauldron. In an instant the great waves rose up foaming, and tossed and dashed against the poor little vessel as if resolved on its destruction. As the storm raged across her the dear *Claymore* heeled over, and quivered as if she had received a blow, but righting herself immediately, she gallantly faced her foe and prepared for another shock. Speedily it came— and again another, and another. More and more furious became the wind, and though the foresail had been reefed, and we had only the storm-jib, it was necessary to furl them both and take in the jib-boom; but in vain the men pulled and strained, the ropes were frozen. Servants, cooks, every man on board was summoned, Mr. Harvey, Captain Martini, and Charlie cheering on the men, as they too sprang forward to the ropes; but crash after crash came the great waves, as they raged against the yacht with a fury that it seemed almost impossible anything of wood and iron could long withstand.

At length Charlie and another man, with their knives between their teeth, crawled on to the bowsprit, though every plunge buried them deep in the waves, and succeeded in severing the ropes that held the sail. Relieved from the too great pressure, the little vessel rose more easily, and we heard a voice say cheerfully, "We shall do now." It was of course impossible to be on deck, but my sister, Mademoiselle G., and I remained crouched on the staircase listening in intense anxiety to the turmoil. When the sail was at last taken in I went down to the children, fearing they would be frightened, but the little creatures had gone to sleep before the gale began, and neither storm nor wind awakened them. It was difficult to stay by them. Exaggerating probably the danger we were in, their lovely, quiet sleep quite unnerved one; so, as it was better to do rather than to think, we busied ourselves as much as possible in making hot tea for those on deck, though even this little task was a work of difficulty, so violently were we thrown from side to side. Occasionally during the night one of us crept up the companion and ventured a hurried look-out.

People have written much about the majestic beauty of a storm. To me it was simply *horrible*. In the distracting rush and confusion, it seemed as if the elements, seized with hideous rage, were tearing and rending each other like infuriated animals. I looked on with the shuddering horror one would feel if standing between wild beasts who were preparing to spring at each other's throats. When holding fast by the sides of the companion I ventured a hurried glance upwards. My heart seemed for a moment to stand still, as I saw a huge black mass, rather than a wave of water, towering high above us. So monstrous, so steep did it seem, that until one felt the vessel rising, it seemed impossible that anything framed by man could surmount so precipitous a wall. Piles of foam rose still higher in the air, which was filled with a pale, ghastly light when the moon showed herself occasionally between the great heavy banks of clouds, as if afraid to look fully forth on such a weird scene of chaos and confusion. But worse even than the sight was the overpowering noise—the uproar. Instead of diminishing as day began to dawn the rush and the roar deepened, until the senses seemed carried away by the mighty clamour, and the brain seemed to whirl, as if it also was the sport of the tremendous wind. Everything was crashing, first on one side, then on the other.

In the midst of this wild turmoil a deep unearthly sound rang through the vessel—the slow, heavy toll of a bell that seemed to come from beneath the sea. For a moment our crew, all Italians, but as brave a set of men as ever trod a deck, seemed paralyzed. Again the warning sound pealed forth; several fell on their knees on receiving as they believed so direct an intimation of our fate.

Mr. Harvey and the captain rushed below, for it was absolutely necessary to ascertain the cause. Happily in their anxious search the ominous sound was again heard as they passed through the galley. Two very large copper pans had got loose, and when the vessel rolled heavily one way, they struck against each other, and the blow produced the solemn clang that had appeared so terrific. Fortunately, therefore, the dark omen became a cause of merriment to our superstitious but light-hearted sailors.

Many a ghost-story, probably, has quite as prosaic an origin.

Before the gale began the evening had been oppressively warm; my window on deck had, therefore, been opened. In the hurry and confusion that ensued when the squall came on, it had been closed, but not securely fastened, and I was suddenly and most disagreeably reminded of the omission. Quite worn out with fatigue and anxiety, I had gone to my cabin to lie down for half an hour, when the yacht made an unusually heavy plunge, and the window burst open, just as a cataract of spray and water poured over the deck. Down came a torrent into my cabin, destroying in a minute all the freshness and coquetry of the pretty lace curtains and pink ribbons, and giving me and all my belongings a thorough bath. A more unpleasant sensation can scarcely be imagined, though a few months' yachting gives one a miserable equanimity about spoiling clothes. Sometimes when a very favourite garment is found covered with a verdant coating of green mould, a few indignant remarks are made upon *sea-damp*; but, generally speaking, any little spirit on the subject, any little vanity is early crushed, and one remains calm in mind and shabby in person to the end of the voyage.

Towards mid-day on Thursday the gale broke a little, that is to say, there were longer intervals between the squalls, but it was an anxious time, for we were off Cape Karempi, and the most dangerous part of the Black Sea navigation lies between this point and Cape Aia on the northern coast. Nearly half the wrecks take place near this cape. The currents are numerous and very strong, and for more than a hundred miles not a harbour nor place of refuge is to be found. Alas! for the luckless vessel which may be driven too near these cruel rocks! Little hope for her in a northerly gale, should this iron-bound coast, with its miles of foaming breakers, come in sight.

Many were the anxious inquiries we made as to our position with reference to this dreaded cape. Happily, we had every reason to believe that we were well out to sea, and the vessel now lay-to, without shipping a drop of water.

Although worn out with fatigue, it was impossible to sleep all Thursday night, so tremendous was the rolling. We were quite black and blue from the bruises we had in consequence of being so tossed from side to side in our cots.

On Friday morning both sea and wind became more moderate, and for many hours we slept the sound sleep of the tired. In the afternoon we bethought ourselves of our unfortunate menagerie, and went to see how the poor creatures had fared during the storm.

The unlucky geese had been the greatest sufferers. Little they thought when they left the peaceful farmyard at Karani of what was in store for them. The water had been so constantly over the fore part of the vessel, and the cold had been so great, that the men had good-naturedly taken the poor things to the forecastle.

One luckless goose, however, either from fright or from having imprudently committed a slight excess in drinking half a bottle of turpentine, had been seized with fits, and remained in an alarming state for many hours. We were much grieved, thinking her last moment had come, for she was lying on her back, feebly kicking in a deplorable fashion, when, with a supreme effort, she dragged herself into the coal-hole, and convulsively began to swallow some bits of coal.

We left in sadness, thinking this could only be the last expiring struggle; but an hour later we received a bulletin to say the patient was not only alive, but better, and in the evening she was pronounced convalescent, her remedy having proved most effectual.

However, between the fits and the coals, our friend presents a lamentable spectacle: the fits have caused her wings to twist inside out, and the coals have given her such a sooty tinge, that not a trace remains of her once beautiful snowy plumage.

We hear that many a candle has been vowed by the men to their favourite shrines. They have behaved admirably; but few of them had ever been in the Black Sea, and none had seen a storm there before.

Even the imperturbable Charlie says he has never known an "uglier" gale. The crew's admiration of the behaviour of the *Claymore* is quite unbounded; they cannot praise her enough. She has certainly weathered the storm gallantly, and has come gloriously out of the combat, without having sustained any injury to speak of—only a rope or two gone and a block broken.

On Saturday morning we were safely anchored off the Water Gate in Sevastopol harbour, and remained there a few days to recruit our somewhat exhausted strength.

Each day brought sad accounts of the numerous wrecks that had taken place in this storm, the most severe that has been known for years.

Amongst other catastrophes, it gave us a great shock to hear of the total loss of the Persian emigrant steamer that we had seen at Sinope. She went down very suddenly early on Thursday morning. A mate and three seamen clung to a spar, were picked up, and brought to Kamiesch. Every other soul on board perished. The men say the vessel was leaky and overladen. It was frightful to think that all those poor creatures we had seen only a few days ago had met with so terrible an end.

The papers are full of the disasters that have taken place.

Before entering the Bosphorus we met the English man-of-war kindly sent by our friends at Constantinople in search of us, for our lengthened absence and the tremendous gale had alarmed them for our safety.

The next day we were at Therapia, perfectly happy, not only in the rest of so charming a haven, but in being once more with most dear and valued friends.

THE END.